Rice Cooker Meals

FAST HOME COOKING FOR BUSY PEOPLE

Jambalayas
Casseroles
Seafood
Pastas
Yams
Soups
Potatoes
Cabbage
Rice Side Dishes

Cypress Cove
Publishing

by NEAL BERTRAND

ACKNOWLEDGEMENTS

We wish to thank:

The wonderful Extension Home Economists with
the Louisiana State University (LSU) AgCenter: Mandy G. Armentor,
Michelle B. Lemoine, Debbie Melvin, Adrienne Vidrine,
Patty Vidrine-Daigle, and Margaret Burlew.
The many good cooks whose recipe contributions appear in this book;
and all the cooks who tested our recipes.
My son Steven Bertrand, who helped create recipes for the book,
for his encouragement and motivation to complete this major project.
Lisa Menard, for helping with the writing, cooking and giving much encouragement.
Doug Dugas, for a beautiful photograph for the front cover.
Sandra Day, for making the food smile for the camera.

• • • • •

Neal Bertrand, Author and Publisher

For information, contact Neal Bertrand at Cypress Cove Publishing, (337) 224-6576.
Visit our website for new items and free recipes at www.RiceCookerMeals.com and
www.CypressCovePublishing.com.
Cypress Cove Publishing
P.O. Box 91626
Lafayette, Louisiana 70509-1626

ISBN-13: 978-0-9705868-4-1
Library of Congress Catalog Card Number: 2007908660

ABOUT THE FRONT COVER This mouth-watering dish of Shrimp Fettuccine is one of many
meals that can be made in your rice cooker. Look for the recipe on page 33.

AUTHOR, EXECUTIVE EDITOR AND PUBLISHER Neal Bertrand
FRONT COVER PHOTOGRAPHY Doug Dugas, Lafayette, Louisiana
SHRIMP FETTUCCINE FOOD STYLING Sandra Day, food stylist, Lafayette, Louisiana
EDITED BY Robin L. Kline, Registered Dietitian and Certified Culinary Professional;
Savvy Food Communications, Des Moines, Iowa
BOOK DESIGN AND PRODUCTION Elizabeth Bell, eBelldesign, Lafayette, Louisiana

PRINTED IN THE USA

CONTENTS

INTRODUCTION

Whether you're a busy mom, a single dad, a college student, an RV enthusiast, a tailgating-before-the-game partier, a senior citizen, or just someone who wants to cook a quick and easy meal that doesn't "heat up" your whole kitchen or use all your pots ... ***Rice Cooker Meals: Fast Home Cooking for Busy People*** is FOR YOU!

Cooking healthy, nutritious, home-cooked meals in our fast-paced society is becoming harder and harder to do. This book can put an end to your household's "fast-food-itis" problem. *Rice Cooker Meals* will quickly become the book that *stays* on the kitchen counter, not filed away on a shelf.

You'll stay as cool as your kitchen does when you use these recipes. You're not firing up your stove or oven. You're not dirtying multiple pots and pans. You're just cooking worry-free, quick meals in record speed! A traditional home-cooked meal – all in one rice cooker. Get ready for a Kitchen Revolution!

PREFACE

WHAT QUALIFIES ME TO WRITE A RICE COOKER COOKBOOK?

THAT'S A GOOD QUESTION!

I am not a chef. I have no culinary training. I am not a "Foodie"... although I do like to eat.

I have not cooked that much in my lifetime. It's not something that I would choose to do. I figure, why cook, when I can open up a can of whatever, nuke it in my microwave, and carry on with my life?

The alternative has always been to be stuck in front of a stove, watching the food so it doesn't burn, and so on. That just seemed to be a little harder than what I wanted to do.

I've been cooking rice in a rice cooker since the 1970s. That's simple.

Then a few years ago I saw a recipe for jambalaya in a rice cooker and I said to myself, "Whoa. I could do that." So I did it, it came out great and I was so excited. I figured, this is a whole new mindset, now! *I* could even do this!

Cooking a delicious one-pot meal in a rice cooker in about 30 minutes, now that's more my speed. Press the cook button and then go watch TV or a video, then eat in a half hour.

So I decided to come up with my own recipes. Meals that, in my opinion, really taste good. Meals that people would actually *want* to eat. So I started on my cooking adventure. I spent a ton of money on ingredients and several months of experimenting, cooking and re-cooking, getting the recipes just right.

I picked ingredients and put them in certain combinations that I thought would taste good, which would work okay and would make a flavorful meal.

So, what qualifies me to write a rice cooker cookbook? Just that I did it myself, experimenting one meal at a time, with the help and encouragement of others, and with feedback from many fine cooks in this State who tested my recipes and blessed me with their wonderful testimonials.

If you see a recipe that you are thinking about passing up because it has too much seasoning or a seasoning you should not have, use the type and amount you are comfortable with. You'll notice throughout this book comments from folks who have tried these recipes. Sometimes they'll give you an idea of how they've adjusted a recipe to suit their taste. You can do that, too.

As you will notice, I am partial to certain ingredients. I like a flavorful meal. I apparently have a higher tolerance for peppery items than some people. (I use Tabasco® as dipping sauce for my grilled chicken.) But feel free to use the spices you want.

Also, I don't care for mushrooms or cream of mushroom soup. If you like them, feel free to add them.

Thanks for trying my recipes.
Please send me comments or testimonials of how you like them.

NEAL BERTRAND, AUTHOR AND PUBLISHER
CYPRESS COVE PUBLISHING

JAMBALAYAS

Black-Eyed Pea & Sausage Jambalaya

This meal is surprisingly good. This is the dish I cooked at the food demonstrations I've done. All who have tasted this dish were very impressed – even the ones who said they didn't care for black-eyed peas.

1 lb. smoked link beef or pork sausage, sliced and browned
1 (15.5-oz.) can black-eyed peas with jalapenos
1 (10.5-oz.) can beef broth
1¼ cups (10 oz.) uncooked medium-grain white rice
1 stick butter, chopped
1 small onion, chopped
1 small bell pepper, chopped
3 cloves garlic, minced
½ cup chopped green onions

Brown the sausage in skillet and drain excess grease. Add all ingredients to rice cooker, stir, cover and press down COOK switch. Once meal is cooked, and the COOK switch pops up to WARM mode, let it stand covered 10 minutes before serving.

Cooked for 18 minutes and made up to the 5-cup level.

REPRINTED FROM *Down-Home Cajun Cooking Favorites*
CYPRESS COVE PUBLISHING, Lafayette, La

• • • • •

"The Black-eyed Pea jambalaya is excellent. Do not change a thing."
MARY JARREAU (FNP PARA-PROFESSIONAL)
LSU AGCENTER, POINTE COUPEE PARISH, NEW ROADS, LA

"We really enjoyed this dish. I used the turkey sausage instead of the beef or pork. I brought some to a friend that I walk with at 6:00 in the morning. By 10:30 that same morning she called me to say how delicious the dish was. She was just going to take a bite, but after one bite she decided to have an early lunch."
PEGGY GISCLAIR - VERMILION PARISH, LA

Black-eyed Pea, Chicken Breast and Turkey Burger Jambalaya

This recipe is a good example of what you can do with a rice cooker. This was my first try at being creative and experimenting with my rice cooker. Having no groceries to eat and starving at 7:00 at night, I scrounged around my empty cabinets and fridge and found enough ingredients to throw together to make a surprisingly delicious meal.

1 (12-oz.) chicken breast, diced
1 turkey burger patty, crumbled
1 tsp. Cajun or Creole seasoning, or to taste
1 tbsp. plus ½ stick butter, chopped
1 (15.5-oz.) can black-eyed peas with jalapenos, with liquid
1 (10-oz.) can diced tomatoes with green chilies, with liquid
1 (8-oz.) can tomato sauce
1 onion, chopped
1 bell pepper, chopped
4 cloves garlic, chopped
2 green onions, chopped
1¼ cups (10 oz.) uncooked medium-grain white rice
1 cup water

Season chicken and turkey with Cajun seasoning; brown in skillet or rice cooker with one tablespoon butter. Add with all remaining ingredients to rice cooker, stir well, cover and press down COOK switch. Once meal is cooked, and the COOK switch pops up to WARM mode, let it stand covered 10-15 minutes before serving.

Cooked for 30 minutes and made up to the 6-cup level.

• • • • •

"I made the jambalaya and it was a delicious meal and makes enough for 6 people. It made a full pot and since we are only 2 people in my house we had enough for 3 meals. I froze the rest and the taste was real good and the recipe was easy to make."
   JANE SIMON - KAPLAN, LA

"This was a bit spicy for me. If I make it again, I will use diced tomatoes without the green chilies. My husband thought it was very good."
   PEGGY GISCLAIR - VERMILION PARISH, LA

Crawfish Jambalaya

Jambalaya (pronounced jahm-buh-LIE-uh) consists of rice, vegetables and the meat or seafood of your choice. It is usually cooked in a black iron pot on the stove for at least an hour. Now, thanks to your rice cooker, you can have a delicious jambalaya of your choice a lot quicker and easier.
NOTE: SHRIMP, FISH OR THE MEAT OF YOUR CHOICE
       MAY BE SUBSTITUTED FOR CRAWFISH.

1 lb. peeled crawfish tails
2½ rice-cooker cups (15-oz.) uncooked medium-grain white rice
1 (10.5-oz.) can chicken broth
1 (8-oz.) can tomato sauce
1 (4-oz.) can mushroom pieces
1 jalapeno pepper, finely chopped
1 medium onion, chopped
1 medium bell pepper, chopped
1 stick butter, chopped
Cajun or Creole seasoning, to taste
TABASCO® Brand Pepper Sauce to taste, or serve at the table
2/3 cup (6 oz.) water

Add all ingredients to rice cooker, stir, cover and press down COOK switch. Once meal is cooked, and the COOK switch pops up to WARM mode, let it stand covered 10 minutes before serving.

Cooked 29 minutes and made up to the 5-cup level.

CONTRIBUTED BY **ELSIE CASTILLE, FCE VOLUNTEER - BREAUX BRIDGE, LA**

• • • • •

"This dish is very good! I substituted original Rotel tomatoes with green chilies in place of the tomato sauce and jalapeno, and my family really enjoyed it! It is very easy and quick to make!"
   LINDA PATTERSON - JENNINGS, LA

"I omitted the jalapeno peppers and added one stalk of celery chopped. This dish was excellent."
   JOYCE FREELAND - GUEYDAN, LA

"This recipe was so good! I shared the recipe with a friend. This is my kind of cooking, and I'm looking forward to the completed cookbook."
   CLAUDETTE BREAUX, TVFC
   LES AMIES DE BURKWALL VFC CLUB - HOUMA, LA

Eggplant, Beef and Shrimp Jambalaya

Tastes great as it is, or you may omit the ground beef and use a full pound of shrimp instead.

½ lb. ground beef, browned
1 tsp. Cajun or Creole seasoning
Salt, to taste
1 lb. eggplant, peeled & diced small
½ lb. shrimp, peeled and deveined
1 (10-oz.) can diced tomatoes with green chilies
1 (10.5-oz.) can beef broth
1½ cups (12 oz.) uncooked medium-grain white rice
1 stick butter, chopped
½ bell pepper, chopped
1 onion, chopped
3 cloves garlic, minced
1 stalk celery, chopped
2 green onions, chopped
TABASCO® Brand Pepper Sauce to taste, or serve at the table
½ cup water

Drain any grease from beef and season with Cajun or Creole seasoning. Add beef and all remaining ingredients to rice cooker, stir, cover and press down COOK switch. Once meal is cooked, and the COOK switch pops up to WARM mode, let it stand covered 10 minutes before serving.

Cooked for 26 minutes and made up to the 6-cup level.

• • • • •

"Followed the recipe using one pound of shrimp. Cooked in an electric skillet and followed the directions. (I didn't have a rice cooker.) Cooked perfectly in about a half hour. Four of us ate it for lunch and each said it was excellent."
MARY ANN SAGRERA, RETIRED EXTENSION AGENT
LSU AGCENTER - CROWLEY, LA.

"This was very good. It tastes similar to an eggplant dressing my mother-in-law makes without tomatoes. The tomatoes enhanced the flavor and she even liked it."
FLO FRITH - ABBEVILLE, LA

Shrimp and Rice Pilaf

Having lived in south Louisiana all my life, I had never heard of pilaf before. I was totally clueless, until I started doing research and creating recipes for this cookbook. I found out that it is a dish in which a grain, such as rice, is generally first browned in oil, and then cooked in a seasoned broth. When I served it to my friends, I did not tell them what it was. They just raved about how good this "Shrimp Jambalaya" tasted! That's right; it tastes just like a jambalaya. See for yourself…shrimp and rice pilaf, Cajun-style.

1 stick butter, chopped
1 cup (8 oz.) uncooked medium-grain white rice
1 lb. shrimp, peeled and deveined
1 (15.5-oz.) can beef broth
1 medium onion, chopped
1 small bell pepper, chopped
1 (7-oz.) can sliced mushrooms, drained
Salt, red & black pepper to taste

Press down COOK switch. Add butter, let it start melting. Add the rice and brown for a few minutes. Add remaining ingredients to rice cooker, stir and cover. Once meal is cooked, and the COOK switch pops up to WARM mode, let it stand covered 10 minutes before serving.

Cooked for 25 minutes and made up to the 3-cup level.

RECIPE FROM **LOUISE LANDRY** - CONTRIBUTED BY **JOSIE THEVIS** - RAYNE, LA

• • • • •

"I used ½ stick butter; I found that to be enough. Served it for supper – the entire family enjoyed it. Delicious, quick and easy!"
ADRIANNE VIDRINE, EXTENSION AGENT - LSU AGCENTER - CROWLEY, LA

"What a quick way to make this dish. It was good, tasty, and colorful. There was none left and my family really enjoyed this recipe. Of course, with rice and seafood you cannot go wrong with my family."
VIRGIE FOREMAN - MAURICE, LA

Shrimp Creole Jambalaya

Shrimp in a tomato gravy with savory vegetables, seasonings and rice...
Wow! Recipe testing is such hard work, but someone has to do it.

1 lb. shrimp, peeled and deveined
2 tsp. Cajun or Creole seasoning, or to taste
1 (10-oz.) can diced tomatoes with green chilies, with liquid
2 tbsp. tomato paste
1½ cups (12 oz.) uncooked medium-grain white rice
1 stick butter, chopped
½ cup chopped green onion
½ green bell pepper, chopped
½ red bell pepper, chopped
2 stalks celery, chopped
4 cloves garlic, minced
1½ cups water
½ cup chopped mushrooms, optional
2 tbsp. Worcestershire sauce

Spray rice pot with non-stick vegetable spray. Add shrimp to rice pot and coat well with seasoning. Add remaining ingredients to rice cooker, stir well, cover and press down COOK switch. Once meal is cooked, and the COOK switch pops up to WARM mode, stir and let it stand covered 10 to 15 minutes before serving.

Cooked for 31 minutes and made up to the 6-cup level.

CONTRIBUTED BY **BELINDA SAVOIE - CROWLEY, LA**

• • • • •

"This is a very good dish. I only used half the garlic. It was great."
RUTH EWING - WELSH, LA

Shrimp Jambalaya

*What a delicious dish! I brought this dish to a get-together and
had many compliments. You may also substitute one pound of fish,
sausage or meat of your choice.*

1 lb. shrimp, peeled and deveined
1 tsp. Cajun or Creole seasoning, or to taste
1 (10-oz.) can diced tomatoes & green chilies
1 (10.5-oz.) can chicken broth
2 cups (16 oz.) uncooked medium-grain white rice
1 stick butter, chopped
1 large onion, chopped
1 bell pepper, chopped
2 ribs celery, chopped
4 cloves garlic, minced
Chopped parsley, to taste
½ cup chopped green onion

Put shrimp in rice cooker, sprinkle seasoning over it and massage it
in thoroughly. Add remaining ingredients to rice cooker, stir well, cover
and press down COOK switch. Once meal is cooked, and the COOK
switch pops up to WARM mode, stir and let it stand covered
10 minutes before serving.

Cooked for 21 minutes and made up to the 6-cup level.

RECIPE BY **JOSEF KORMESSER**
CONTRIBUTED BY **PATTY VIDRINE-DAIGLE, HOME ECONOMIST**
LSU AGCENTER - JENNINGS, LA

· · · · ·

"A super easy and quick dish that was very tasty. I would prepare it again and add a little
more seasoning and mushrooms."
   BETTY MILLER - CROWLEY, LA

Shrimp Opelousas

Here's another variation of Shrimp Jambalaya. Feel free to omit the mushrooms if you wish... I did. Sorry, but I don't care for mushrooms. I'm not a big fan of Cream of Mushroom soup, either. I usually substitute Cream of Celery in its place. You may also substitute fish or crawfish for shrimp.

1 lb. raw shrimp, peeled and deveined
1 tsp. Cajun or Creole seasoning, or to taste
1 (10-oz.) can diced tomatoes with green chilies
1 (4-oz.) can sliced mushrooms, drained (optional)
1½ cups (12 oz.) uncooked medium-grain white rice
½ stick butter, chopped
1 medium onion, chopped
1 bell pepper, chopped
½ cup chopped green onion
Parsley, to taste
9 oz. water

Put shrimp in rice cooker, sprinkle seasoning over it and massage it in thoroughly. Add remaining ingredients to rice cooker, stir well, cover and press down COOK switch. Once meal is cooked, and the COOK switch pops up to WARM mode, stir and let it stand covered 10 minutes before serving.

Cooked for 32 minutes and made up to the 6-cup level.

CONTRIBUTED BY **BELINDA SAVOIE - CROWLEY, LA**

• • • • •

"I brought this to a family get together and everyone liked it."
FLO FRITH - ABBEVILLE, LA

MEATS

Ball Park "Casserole"

Bring this ball park favorite home. Chili and corn chips in the comfort of your own home – all in your rice cooker!

1 lb. ground beef
1 (10-oz.) can diced tomatoes with green chilies
1 (14.75-oz.) can cream style corn
1 medium onion, chopped
3 cloves garlic, minced
¼ cup sliced black olives
Salt & pepper, to taste
2 tbsp. chili powder
¾ cup water
1 (8-oz.) package shredded Colby/Monterey Jack cheese
3 cups corn chips

Brown the meat in rice cooker or skillet, then add all ingredients to rice cooker except cheese and chips, stir, cover and press down COOK switch. Once meal is cooked, and the COOK switch pops up to WARM mode, add cheese and chips, stir well to coat, cover for five minutes, then serve.

NOTE: IF YOU WOULD RATHER NOT ADD THE CHIPS TO THE POT, YOU
COULD PUT THE FOOD IN A BOWL AND ADD THE CORN CHIPS TO
YOUR BOWL, OR SCOOP THE FOOD WITH THE CHIPS. MANY PEOPLE
WOULD NOT WANT TO PUT THE CHIPS IN THE RICE POT AND LET
IT SIT FOR LONG BECAUSE IT WILL MAKE THE CHIPS SOGGY.

Cooked for 18 minutes and made up to the 5-cup level before adding chips.

· · · · ·

"The Ball Park Casserole is easy to make and the chips really give a little crunch. I suggest serving right after adding the chips and cheese. That way the chips do not have time to soften."
MARY JARREAU, FNP PARAPROFESSIONAL - LSU AGCENTER
POINTE COUPEE PARISH - NEW ROADS, LA

Cajun Pepper Steak

To be served over hot rice or pasta. Or as an added treat, make a Cajun Pepper Steak Baked Stuffed Potato. Either bake a potato or use the recipe for our Stuffed Potatoes in the Vegetables chapter, and mix this steak dish into it. Awesome!

1 lb. boneless round steak, cut into bite-size pieces
1 tbsp. olive oil
1 (.87-oz.) envelope Brown Gravy Mix
1 (10.5-oz.) can beef broth
1 (10-oz.) can diced tomatoes with green chilies
½ large onion, chopped
½ bell pepper, chopped
5 garlic cloves, minced
2 tsp. Worcestershire sauce
1/8 tsp. dried bay leaf flakes
½ tsp. dried basil
½ tsp Cajun or Creole seasoning
TABASCO® Brand Pepper Sauce to taste, or serve at the table
Hot, cooked rice

Brown the meat in olive oil in skillet and keep the gravy. Make one cup of the Gravy Mix in a separate small saucepan. Add all ingredients to rice cooker except rice, stir, cover and press down COOK switch. Once meal is cooked, and the COOK switch pops up to WARM mode, serve immediately.

Cooked for 40 minutes and made up to the 2-cup level.

· · · · ·

"Very tasty. Next time I cook it I'll leave the bay leaf out altogether. Some said they found it a little too seasoned. Instead of serving over rice, possibly mix with rice and serve 'jambalaya-style.'"
JEANETTE CROCHET - JENNINGS, LA

Cajalian Chicken Cacciatore

"Cajalian" cuisine (Cajun/Italian) blends the distinct tastes of Cajun food, with its spicy flavor and roux, with Italian food, with its unmistakable layering of tomato sauce, Italian seasonings, garlic, and cheese. It's the best of "both worlds!"

3 boneless, skinless chicken breasts, cubed into small pieces
Salt and red pepper, to taste
Garlic powder, to taste
Mixed Italian seasonings, to taste
1 bag of Seasoning Blend (chopped onions, bell peppers, etc.
   - found in frozen vegetables section)
1 (8-oz.) can tomato sauce
5 tbsp. Tony Chachere's Dry Roux Mix dissolved in
   1 cup cool water
1 cup chopped fresh mushrooms (optional)
Parmesan cheese, to taste
A pinch of sugar, or to taste, to balance acid in tomato sauce
Hot, cooked rice

Brown chicken breasts in a skillet or rice cooker and season well with salt and red pepper. Add all ingredients to rice cooker, stir, cover and press down COOK switch. Cook until chicken is tender, stirring once or twice during cooking time, then covering again. Once meal is cooked, and the COOK switch pops up to WARM mode, serve immediately over rice.

Serves 4 - 6.

CONTRIBUTED BY **LISA LANZA-MENARD - LAFAYETTE, LA**

• • • • •

"I omitted the Italian seasoning and tomato sauce and substituted for it the Italian Style diced tomatoes. Instead of the chicken breasts I used deboned chicken thighs and drumsticks. I also added ½ cup chopped parsley and onion tops. This is a very good recipe and I love to cook in my rice cooker. Your rice pot recipes are very good and promote the rice industry and I really appreciate it since we are rice farmers. I wish to thank you for promoting rice."

JOYCE FREELAND - GUEYDAN, LA

Cajalian Chicken Cacciatore Alfredo

Cajalian Chicken Cacciatore
1 jar Alfredo Sauce

This dish is a delicious variation of the Cajalian Chicken Cacciatore. Prepare "Cajalian Chicken Cacciatore" according to its recipe (you can add more chicken if you'd like, since this dish will serve 6 - 8). When the dish is done, add one half to one whole jar of your favorite ready-made Alfredo sauce (can be found by the spaghetti sauces at your grocer), and stir until blended well. A whole jar will make the sauce very light in color and the Alfredo taste will be more prominent, but with the Cajalian "kick." If you add a half jar or so of the Alfredo sauce, it will be a darker Alfredo with more of a blended taste between the two dishes.

Serve over angel hair pasta, or the pasta of your choice. Delicious!

Serves 6 - 8.

CONTRIBUTED BY **LISA LANZA-MENARD - LAFAYETTE, LA**

• • • • •

Mexican Taco "Casserole" I

Here's another great-tasting Mexican dish. It can also be made into a Stuffed Potato, but without the chips. See our Stuffed Potatoes recipes in the Vegetables chapter.

2 lbs. lean ground beef
1 (15-oz.) can enchilada sauce
1 (10.5-oz.) can cream of celery condensed soup
1 onion, chopped
Salt and pepper, to taste
1 tsp. chili powder
¼ tsp. turmeric
1/3 cup water
1 (15.25-oz.) jar salsa con queso cheese dip
1 (13-oz.) bag nacho cheese chips, crushed

Brown the meat in a skillet; remove extra liquid. Add browned beef and all remaining ingredients, except for cheese dip and chips, to rice cooker, stir well, cover and press down COOK switch. Cook at least 25 to 30 minutes. If rice cooker stops prematurely, wait a while, then press down COOK switch again. Once meal has cooked, and the COOK switch pops up to WARM mode, drain any excess liquid, add cheese dip and enough chips to suit your taste, and stir.

This meal is great as a dip, to make Stuffed Potatoes, or over hot rice.

NOTE: YOU MAY CHOOSE TO NOT ADD THE CHIPS TO THE POT, BUT RATHER TO SERVE THE CHIPS SEPARATELY AT THE TABLE SO THEY DON'T GET SOGGY.

Cooked for 25 minutes and made up to the 5.5-cup level.

· · · · ·

"I made the Mexican Taco Casserole and served it as a dip and put the extra chips around my dish and they did not get soggy. Everyone enjoyed it and I had never used tumeric before and it gives it a very good taste."
   ROMONA BABINEAUX - ERATH, LA

"I made this as a dip and everyone loved it. I added jalapenos because we like things hot!"
   FLO FRITH - ABBEVILLE, LA

Mexican Taco "Casserole" II

Here's a variation of our other Taco Casserole dish. ¡Delicioso!

1 lb. ground meat (beef or turkey), browned
Salt, pepper and other seasonings of your choice
1 (4-oz.) can chopped green chilies
1 (10-oz.) can diced tomatoes with green chilies
1 (10.5-oz.) can beef broth
1 (1.5-oz.) envelope taco seasoning
1 (1.25-oz.) envelope chili seasoning
1 medium onion, chopped
½ cup water
2 cups Mexican-style shredded cheese
½ of a 13-oz. bag nacho cheese flavored tortilla chips

Brown the meat in a skillet, drain excess liquid, and then season the meat well with salt and pepper. Add all ingredients to rice cooker except for cheese and chips, stir, cover and press down COOK switch. Once meal is cooked, and the COOK switch pops up to WARM mode, quickly add cheese and chips, stirring each well to blend in and cover to allow cheese to melt. Let it stand covered 10 minutes before serving.

NOTE: YOU MAY CHOOSE TO NOT ADD THE CHIPS TO THE POT, BUT RATHER TO SERVE THE CHIPS SEPARATELY AT THE TABLE SO THEY DON'T GET SOGGY.

Cooked for 27 minutes and made up to the 5-cup level.

· · · · ·

Red Beans and Rice

At most of the "plate lunch" places in south Louisiana, this simple but tasty dish is special enough to serve once a week. For some, nothing else is better.

1 lb. smoked beef or pork sausage
1 (15.5-oz.) can red beans, undrained
1 (15.5-oz.) can chili beans, undrained
1 (10.5-oz.) can beef broth
1 bell pepper, chopped
1 onion, chopped
1 green onion, chopped
3 cloves garlic, minced
½ tsp. Cajun or Creole seasoning
TABASCO® Brand Pepper Sauce to taste, or serve at the table
½ cup water
Hot, cooked rice

Slice sausage in small pieces and brown in skillet or rice cooker; drain grease. Add all ingredients to rice cooker except rice, stir, cover and press down COOK switch. Once meal is cooked, and the COOK switch pops up to WARM mode, serve immediately over hot rice.

Cooked for 52 minutes and made up to 5-cup level.

· · · · ·

"Great Cajun classic at its best! The seasoning balance was pleasing to my taste. The ease of preparation is a real plus – just mix, hit the switch and before you know it, it's ready to serve."
   RENA V. LABAT - TOWN AND COUNTRY VFC CLUB - HOUMA, LA

Sausage Sauce Piquante

Here's a basic sauce piquante (pronounced pee-KAHNT) dish that I made with sausage. It can be made with any kind of meat or seafood. It is usually eaten over hot, fluffy rice, but this is another dish that would taste great mixed in with baked or rice cooker potatoes; see the Stuffed Potatoes recipes in the Vegetables chapter.

1 lb. smoked sausage, cut in small pieces
1 (6-oz.) can tomato paste
1 (8-oz.) can tomato sauce
1 (10-oz.) can diced tomatoes with green chilies
1 large onion, chopped
4 cloves garlic, minced
1 bell pepper, chopped
½ cup chopped green onion
Parsley, to taste
Salt and pepper, to taste
1½ cups water
Hot rice or potatoes

Brown sausage in a skillet and drain grease. Add all ingredients to rice cooker except rice, stir, cover and press down COOK switch. Once meal is cooked, and the COOK switch pops up to WARM mode, serve over rice.

Cooked for 40 minutes and made up to 3-cup level.

· · · · ·

"I added ½ cup chopped parsley. Used turkey sausage and I did not add salt and pepper, and we found it to be okay without it. I served it to three elderly ladies – one found it a little too tomato-ey, but the other two said it was good. The general consensus: 'Ummm, this is GOOD!'"
   ROSIE TRAHAN, PRESIDENT
   VOLUNTEERS FOR FAMILY & COMMUNITY (VFC) NIGHT CLUB - CROWLEY, LA

Steven's Easy Chili

My son Steven created this recipe the traditional way on the stove when he was twelve years old. He's been wowing guests and family with it ever since. Now he has perfected it to work in your rice cooker.

1 lb. ground beef, browned
1 (1.25-oz.) envelope Chili Seasoning Mix
1 (15.5-oz.) can small red chili beans in spicy tomato sauce
1 (10-oz.) can diced tomatoes with green chilies
¼ tsp. Cajun or Creole seasoning
½ tsp. garlic powder
½ tsp. onion powder
1 cup water

After browning meat in skillet, add all ingredients to rice cooker, stir, cover and press down COOK switch. Once meal is cooked, and the COOK switch pops up to WARM mode, let it stand covered 10 minutes before serving.

Cooked for 36 minutes and made up to the 3-cup level.

CONTRIBUTED BY **STEVEN BERTRAND - LAFAYETTE, LA**

· · · · ·

Stuffed Beef Roast

What? Cooking a roast in a rice cooker?
My friend Kim has been cooking roasts in her rice pot for years.
I ate some and it was so good! Try it.

2.4-lb. beef roast, seasoned
6 cloves garlic, minced
1 medium onion, chopped
Seasonings

Season the outside of the roast according to your taste. In a food processor, chop garlic and onion, add your favorite pepper and seasoning to it, cut slits in the roast, and then stuff the roast with some of the mixture (reserve any remaining mixture). Place roast and 1 ½ cups water in rice cooker. Cook for 1 ½ hours then turn cooker off.

Flip the roast over, it should be turning brown. Add 1 ½ cups water, wait a few minutes for the pot to cool, and then press down the COOK switch. (It won't let you turn it back on right away.) Cook for an hour, and then turn off cooker again.

Flip the roast over again, add 1 ½ cups water (depending on how much gravy you want) any remaining onion and garlic mixture,and scrape the browned meat off the bottom of pot. Turn pot on for another 20 minutes or so, then flip the cooker to WARM setting and serve.

Cooked in a 5-cup rice cooker. Cook time about 3 hours.

CONTRIBUTED BY **KIM DOUCET - CROWLEY, LA**

• • • • •

PASTA

Cheesy Noodle Goulash

What a cheesy treat!

1½ cups water
1 tbsp. olive oil
2 cups egg noodles, uncooked
1 lb. ground beef, browned, drained
Salt & pepper, to taste
1 tsp. chili powder
1 (8-oz.) can tomato sauce
1 (10-oz.) can diced tomatoes with green chilies
1 onion, chopped
3 garlic cloves, minced
TABASCO® Brand Pepper Sauce to taste, or serve at the table
¼-lb. block of processed cheese cut in pieces

Put noodles in rice cooker with water and oil, stir well to coat noodles with oily water to keep them from clumping together.

Add all ingredients to rice cooker except cheese, stir, cover and press down COOK switch. Once meal is cooked, and the COOK switch pops up to WARM mode, add cheese, stir well to mix, and then serve.

Cooked for 30 minutes and made up to the 4-cup level.

· · · · ·

"I found the Cheesy Noodle Goulash tasty and it cooked up nicely."
  MONICA OLINDE, FAMILY AND CONSUMER SCIENCES AGENT
  LSU AGCENTER - POINTE COUPEE PARISH - NEW ROADS, LA

Chicken and Cheesy Macaroni

"Kids" of all ages will love this one.

1¼ cups elbow macaroni, uncooked
1 cup water
1 tbsp. olive oil
1 lb. chicken breast, or your favorite parts,
   cut into bite-size pieces
½ large bell pepper, chopped
1 small onion, chopped
1 (10.5-oz.) can cream of celery soup
1 (10.5-oz.) can chicken broth
Salt and pepper, to taste
1 (8-oz.) package shredded sharp Cheddar cheese

Put macaroni in a bowl with water and oil, stir well to coat with oil. Brown chicken in rice cooker or skillet; add remaining ingredients (except cheese) to chicken in rice cooker, stir, cover and press down COOK switch. Once meal is cooked, and the COOK switch pops up to WARM mode, add cheese, stir well until melted and serve immediately.

Cooked for 24 minutes and made up to the 5-cup level.

· · · · ·

"This recipe was very good. My family and I enjoyed it. It is a fast recipe to prepare. I used a deli chicken not only for quickness, but I could combine white and dark meat without the use of another pan. I would suggest spraying the rice cooker pot with a non-stick cooking spray as some of it stuck to the bottom of the pot. (It may have been my rice cooker). I would also suggest that after mixing the cheese in, to pour it all into a serving dish and soak one's rice pot right away. I used a low-carb elbow macaroni, fat-free, low sodium chicken broth and 2% milk, and sharp Cheddar because of family diets. When I do this dish again, I plan to use two different colored bell peppers to add color to the dish."
BEVERLY REYNAUD - LES AMIES DE BURKWALL - TERREBONNE VFC

Chicken and Pasta

A savory and quick meal!

1½ cups water
1 tbsp. olive oil
2 cups large elbow macaroni, uncooked
1 lb. chicken breast, or your favorite chicken parts,
    cut in bite-size pieces
Salt and pepper, to taste
1 (10-oz.) can diced tomatoes with green chilies
1 (8-oz.) can tomato sauce
1 stick butter, chopped
½ large bell pepper, chopped
1 onion, chopped
3 cloves garlic, chopped
¼ lb. block of processed cheese cut in pieces

Add water and oil to bowl and stir. Add macaroni to liquid and coat well to avoid clumping. Season chicken pieces well and brown in skillet. Add browned chicken and all remaining ingredients, except cheese, to rice cooker, stir, cover and press down COOK switch. Once meal is cooked, and the COOK switch pops up to WARM mode, add cheese, stir well to mix, and then serve.

Cooked for 24 minutes and made up to the 4.5-cup level.

· · · · ·

"This was awesome! I didn't have the elbow macaroni so I used bowtie pasta instead, and it worked great. The whole family loved it. My kids are begging me to make more."
    ANGIE C. - CARENCRO, LA

Chicken Breast and Turkey Sausage Pastalaya

You've heard of jambalaya, right? This is the simplest version of traditional jambalaya, but with a twist... pasta instead of rice!
Hence the name...pastalaya.

Non-stick vegetable cooking spray
1 (10.5-oz.) can beef broth
½ cup water
1 tbsp. olive oil
2 cups elbow macaroni, uncooked
½ lb. chicken breast, sliced into bite-size pieces
½ lb. (1½ links) turkey sausage, sliced into small pieces
Cajun or Creole seasoning, to taste
TABASCO® Brand Pepper Sauce to taste, or serve at the table
½ stick butter, chopped
1 (10-oz.) can diced tomatoes with green chilies
1 onion, chopped fine
½ bell pepper, chopped fine
5 cloves garlic, minced

Spray rice pot with non-stick cooking spray. Add broth, water and oil to a bowl or rice pot and stir. Add macaroni to liquid and coat well to keep from clumping together.

Coat the chicken and sausage with Cajun seasoning; brown for 10 minutes in rice cooker or skillet. Add all ingredients to rice cooker, stir, cover and press down COOK switch. Once meal is cooked, and the COOK switch pops up to WARM mode, serve immediately.

It cooked for 20 minutes and made up to the 4-cup level.

Thanks to Debbie Melvin of the LSU AgCenter for the idea for this recipe, which I modified to make it easier.

• • • • •

"My co-worker tried this recipe and brought it to work. It was a big hit! It was so good. The flavors blended just right, nothing was over-powering."
LETHA VINCENT - CROWLEY, LA

Crawfish or Shrimp Fettuccine

*A classic Cajun dish that can easily be done
in your rice cooker in 35 minutes!*

NOTE: THE DICED TOMATOES WITH GREEN CHILIES AND THE CHEESE DIP BOTH HAVE
A LITTLE PEPPER FLAVOR, SO GO EASY ON ADDING EXTRA PEPPER. SHRIMP MAY
BE SUBSTITUTED IF CRAWFISH ARE NOT AVAILABLE.

1½ cups water
1 tbsp. olive oil
1 (12-oz. box) fettuccine noodles, broken into thirds
1 (10-oz.) can diced tomatoes with green chilies
1 (10.5-oz.) can chicken broth
½ stick butter, chopped
1 lb. peeled crawfish tails
1 onion, chopped fine
½ large bell pepper, chopped fine
5 cloves garlic, minced
½ cup chopped green onion
½ tsp. dried parsley
¼ tsp. Cajun or Creole seasoning
1 (15-oz.) jar salsa con queso cheese dip, "medium" flavor

Put water and olive oil in pot, stir well. Add fettuccine noodles and mix well
in oily water to help prevent sticking together. Add all ingredients to rice
cooker, except cheese dip, stir well, cover and press down COOK switch.
Once meal is cooked, and the COOK switch pops up to WARM mode,
add cheese dip, mix well, and serve hot.

Cooked for 35 minutes and made up to the 6-cup level.

• • • • •

"Used a non-stick, 8-cup rice cooker. This dish is really good! Noodles stuck on bottom of
rice pot and were a bit discolored, but not hard or burned. Perhaps stirring it a bit might
prevent this."
   OLLIE TIETJE - ROANOKE, LA

"I made the fettuccine with crawfish and my whole family loved it!"
   LOU TOUCHET - KAPLAN, LA

Hearty Corn and Black-eyed Pea Pastalaya

This is a unique dish that won't disappoint.

1½ cups water
1 tsp. olive oil
2½ cups elbow macaroni, uncooked
1 lb. ground beef, browned in skillet, drained
Salt, black and red pepper, to taste
1 (15.25-oz.) can whole kernel corn, undrained
1 (15.5-oz.) can black-eyed peas, undrained
1 (10-oz.) can diced tomatoes with green chilies
1 (10.5-oz.) can beef broth
1 (10.5-oz.) can cream of celery soup
½ bell pepper, chopped
1 onion, chopped
3 cloves garlic, minced
1 tsp. onion powder
1 tsp. garlic powder
TABASCO® Brand Pepper Sauce to taste, or serve at the table

Pour water and olive oil in rice cooker and stir well. Add macaroni to water/oil mixture and stir to coat well to prevent clumping together in pot. Season browned beef with salt and peppers; place in rice cooker. Add all remaining ingredients to rice cooker, stir, cover and press down COOK switch. Once meal is cooked, and the COOK switch pops up to WARM mode, serve immediately.

Cooked for 41 minutes and made up to the 8-cup level.

• • • • •

"The vegetables, corn, peas with the macaroni and tomatoes are all favorites of mine.
I also add elbow macaroni to my vegetable soup as my mother used to do.
Loved this recipe and will definitely make it again."
  MARY HILL - LES AMIES DE BURKWALL - TERREBONNE VFC

Pizza Pastalaya

No need to call the pizza man tonight!
This one will get your family's attention.

2 lbs. lean ground beef, browned, drained
Salt and pepper, to taste
1 (10-oz.) can beef broth
1 cup water
1 tbsp. olive oil
2 cups elbow macaroni, uncooked
1 (14-oz.) jar spaghetti sauce
1 (14-oz.) jar pizza sauce
4 oz. pepperoni slices
1 medium onion, chopped
3 cloves garlic, minced
1 small bell pepper, chopped
TABASCO® Brand Pepper Sauce to taste, or serve at the table
Shredded Mozzarella cheese

Season browned beef with salt and pepper. Add broth, water and oil to rice cooker with seasoned beef and stir. Add macaroni to liquid and stir thoroughly to coat well to keep macaroni from clumping together. Add all remaining ingredients to rice cooker except cheese, stir, cover and press down COOK switch. Once meal is cooked, and the COOK switch pops up to WARM mode, stir and serve. Add cheese on top of each serving.

Cooked 21 minutes and made up to the 5 or 6-cup level.

• • • • •

"Taste was good. I added about one teaspoon Tabasco® Sauce. Easy to make and cooked fast... about 35 minutes. Good for a quick after work or church meal.
Very tasty!"
   SANDY MEYER - WELSH, LA.

Spaghetti and Meatballs

A traditional family favorite made easy. For convenience, buy the two-pound bag of 32 flame broiled, Italian Style meatballs found in the frozen foods section of the supermarket. They work great. This classic Italian dish is super easy and super tasty!

12 frozen cooked meatballs
1 (16-oz.) jar spaghetti sauce
1 (7-oz.) box spaghetti, broken in thirds
1 tbsp. olive oil
1 onion, chopped
3 cloves garlic, minced
½ cup chopped green onion
½ cup chopped parsley
Salt, black & red pepper, to taste
1 tsp. oregano
2 cups water

Add all ingredients to rice cooker; stir well to coat spaghetti, cover and press down COOK switch. Once meal is cooked, and the COOK switch pops up to WARM mode, serve immediately.

Cooked for 28 minutes and made up to the 5-cup level.

· · · · ·

"This was good!"
JOY BISSEN - DE SOTO, WI

"I served this recipe to my family this past weekend. I was pleasantly surprised to find that it was so easy to fix. The ingredients are readily available and easy to prepare. The 28 minute cook time really developed a tasty meal. The only objection I have is that the spaghetti noodles were over cooked to my taste."
MARGARET GRAFFEO - ABBEVILLE, LA

Tex-Mex Pasta

Pasta with a Tex-Mex twist!

1 lb. ground beef, browned
Salt, red and black pepper, to taste
1 (12-oz.) box pasta
2 cups water
1 tbsp. olive oil
1 (10-oz.) can diced tomatoes with green chilies
1 (8-oz.) can tomato sauce
1 (10.5-oz.) can beef broth
1 tsp. onion powder
1 tsp. garlic powder
2 tsp. chili powder
1 tsp. cumin
TABASCO® Brand Pepper Sauce to taste, or serve at the table

While browning beef in skillet, season with salt and pepper. Put pasta in rice cooker containing water and olive oil; stir thoroughly to coat pasta well to keep from sticking together. Add remaining ingredients to rice cooker, stir, cover and press down COOK switch. Once meal is cooked, and the COOK switch pops up to WARM mode, serve immediately.

It cooked for 37 minutes and made up to the 5-cup level.

· · · · ·

"Mmm-mmm Good! This spicy dish will become a great family favorite."
    MARGARET & TOOTSIE BURLEW - HOUMA, LA

Zucchini, Butter Beans and Pasta

What a superb and smooth combination.
The flavors meld together for a scrumptious meal.

1 (10.5-oz.) can chicken broth
½ cup water
1 tbsp. olive oil
2 cups elbow macaroni
1 zucchini, peeled and diced
1 (16-oz.) can large butter beans
1 (10-oz.) can diced tomatoes with green chilies
1 medium onion, chopped
½ tsp. Cajun seasoning
TABASCO® Brand Pepper Sauce to taste, or serve at the table

Add broth, water and oil to rice cooker and stir. Add macaroni to liquid and stir thoroughly to coat well. Add remaining ingredients to rice cooker, stir well, cover and press down COOK switch. Once meal is cooked, and the COOK switch pops up to WARM mode, serve immediately.

It cooked for 28 minutes and made up to the 6-cup level.

• • • • •

"The Zucchini, Butter Beans and Pasta tasted great,
but it is a bit too spicy for my taste."
LETA TOUCHET - KAPLAN, LA

RICE SIDE DISHES

Chicken Fried Rice

I tried to duplicate this rice dish that I love so much at my favorite Chinese restaurants. I'm very pleased with the way it came out. This is a quick and easy Oriental dish. The ultimate "take out" while staying in!

2 tbsp. butter
1 egg, beaten
½ cup uncooked chicken breast chopped in small pieces
Salt and pepper, to taste
2 rice-cooker cups (12-oz.) uncooked medium-grain white rice
1 (10.5-oz.) can chicken broth
2 tbsp. soy sauce
½ cup chopped onion
3 green onions, chopped
½ cup chopped baby carrots
½ cup frozen sweet peas, thawed
1 tbsp. grated ginger root, optional
¼ cup water

NOTE: HAVE EVERYTHING PREPPED AND READY BEFORE
      PUTTING ANYTHING IN THE COOKER.

Press down COOK switch. Put butter in rice cooker, let it melt some. Scramble egg in butter, stirring constantly to break it in tiny pieces. Season chicken with salt and pepper, add it to pot and brown for five minutes, turning often to brown thoroughly. Add rice and stir fry into the butter. Add remaining ingredients; stir well and cover. Once meal is cooked, and the COOK switch pops up to WARM mode, let it stand covered 10 minutes before serving.

Cooked for 16 minutes once covered, and made up to the 3-cup level.

· · · · ·

"Perfect! My favorite. We doubled the batch and it turned out fine."
   JOY BISSEN - DE SOTO, WI

"I have tried to duplicate several Chinese dishes, but have not been able to do so until now. This recipe is easy to put together and is so quick to cook. My family wants this at least once a week."
   MARGARET GRAFFEO - ABBEVILLE, LA

Dark Rice

Coconut, coke, raisins and nuts: Not what you'd expect for a rice side dish. This one will surprise you!

2 rice-cooker cups (12 oz.) uncooked medium-grain white rice
1 cup (8 oz.) water
1 cup (8 oz.) cola
1 tsp. olive oil
¼ tsp. salt, or to taste
¾ cup golden raisins
2/3 cup sweet shredded coconut flakes
½ cup chopped pecans, or nuts of your choice
½ cup chopped green onions

Place the rice, water, cola, oil and salt in rice cooker. Stir, cover and press down COOK switch. At the midpoint of cooking process, 10 minutes, quickly toss in the raisins and cover. Once meal is cooked, and the COOK switch pops up to WARM mode, add coconut, nuts and green onion and mix well. Cover and let it stand 10 minutes before serving. This dish is excellent to accompany pork or chicken.

Cooked for 21 minutes and made up to the 4-cup level.

· · · · ·

CONTRIBUTED BY **ELSIE H. CASTILLE, FCE VOLUNTEER - BREAUX BRIDGE, LA**

Lemon Pepper Rice

This one's a real winner! Flavorful and fluffy!

3 rice-cooker cups (18 oz.) uncooked medium-grain white rice
1 medium onion, chopped
½ bell pepper, chopped
1 jalapeno pepper, seeded and chopped
¼ cup of chopped celery
4 tbsp. pimento
1 stick butter, chopped
1 (7-oz.) can sliced mushrooms, drained
3 tbsp. lemon pepper
3 cups water

Add all ingredients to rice cooker, stir, cover and press down COOK switch. Once meal is cooked, and the COOK switch pops up to WARM mode, let it stand covered 10 minutes before serving.

I adapted the original stovetop recipe version, contributed by Mrs. Lorraine Bertrand, of Bertrand Rice Farm in Elton, LA, to work in your rice cooker.

Cooked 31 minutes and made up to the 5-cup level.

• • • • •

"This dish is so easy and flavorful. An excellent side dish with fish or pork."
MARY SAMAHA - HOMEMAKERS HOLIDAY VFC CLUB - HOUMA, LA

Lemony Rice

This dish is great alone, but also can be used as a base for mixing in your own ingredients. Be creative … last night's leftovers?

Vegetable cooking spray
1 (8-oz.) cup uncooked medium-grain white rice
1 tsp. butter
1 clove garlic, minced
1 tsp. grated lemon peel
¼ tsp. black pepper
2 tbsp. snipped parsley
1 1/3 cup chicken broth
1/3 cup water

Spray rice cooker pot with cooking spray. Add all ingredients to rice cooker, stir, cover and press down COOK switch. Once meal is cooked, and the COOK switch pops up to WARM mode, let it stand covered 10 minutes before serving.

Cooked for 20 minutes and made up to the 1.5-cup level.

CONTRIBUTED BY **RIVIANA RICE**

· · · · ·

"I cooked this lemony rice recipe and liked it."
MONICA OLINDE, FAMILY AND CONSUMER SCIENCES AGENT
LSU AGCENTER
POINTE COUPEE PARISH - NEW ROADS, LA

Mexican Rice

Easy and ethnic – all in the same pot! ¡Sabroso!

1 ¼ cups (10 oz.) uncooked medium-grain white rice
3 tbsp. butter, divided
½ cup chopped onion
¼ cup chopped bell pepper
1 clove garlic, minced
1 ½ cups water
1 (10-oz.) can diced tomatoes with green chilies
½ tsp. salt
2 tsp. chili powder

Press down COOK switch. Put one tablespoon butter in cooker, and let it melt; add rice, let it brown, stirring constantly. Add remaining butter and all ingredients, stir well and cover. Once meal is cooked, and the COOK switch pops up to WARM mode, let it stand covered 10 minutes before serving.

Cooked for 26 minutes and made up to the 3-cup level.

CONTRIBUTED BY **MONICA OLINDE, FCS AGENT**
LSU AGCENTER-POINTE COUPEE PARISH

• • • • •

"Excellent! The boys loved it."
JOY BISSEN - DE SOTO, WI

"An easy recipe to put together. The end product is very colorful and tasty."
BEVERLY REYNAUD
LES AMIES DE BURKWALL - TERREBONNE VFC

Mushroom Rice

If you like mushrooms, you'll love this version!

1 (7-oz.) can mushrooms, drained
1¼ cups (10 oz.) uncooked medium-grain white rice
1 (10.5-oz.) can chicken broth
¾ stick butter, chopped
1 large purple onion, chopped
Salt, red & black pepper, to taste

Add all ingredients to rice cooker, stir, cover and press down COOK switch. Once meal is cooked, and the COOK switch pops up to WARM mode, let it stand covered 10 minutes before serving.

Cooked 27 minutes and made up to the 2½-cup level.

CONTRIBUTED BY **WILLIE MAE DAILEY - CROWLEY, LA**

• • • • •

"This was a tasty dish to eat after working all day. I think it would make a good side dish to eat with seafood. I usually don't care for mushrooms but I enjoyed it."
   AL THIBODEAUX - ARNAUDVILLE, LA

"I loved it! This is wonderful as a side dish."
   MARY SAMAHA - HOMEMAKERS HOLIDAY VFC CLUB - HOUMA, LA

Mushroom-Jalapeno Rice

This dish is the perfect complement for chicken, beef, pork or fish. It's on the mild side, so kick in another jalapeno to spice it up according to your palate.

1½ cups (12 oz.) uncooked medium-grain white rice
1 stick butter, chopped
1 (10.5-oz.) can cream of chicken soup or
    1 (10.5-oz.) can of chicken broth
1 (4-oz.) can sliced mushrooms, drained
1 bell pepper, chopped
1 small onion, chopped
1 jalapeno pepper, seeded & chopped
1 tsp. salt
1 tsp. garlic powder

Add all ingredients to rice cooker, stir, cover and press down COOK switch. Once meal is cooked, and the COOK switch pops up to WARM mode, let it stand covered 10 minutes before serving.

Cooked for about 30 minutes and made up to the 3-cup level.

CONTRIBUTED BY **PATTY VIDRINE-DAIGLE, HOME ECONOMIST**
LSU AGCENTER - JENNINGS, LA

· · · · ·

"Good! Good!! Good!!!"
    MARY SAMAHA - HOMEMAKERS HOLIDAY VFC CLUB - HOUMA, LA.

Pecan Rice

Nutty rice – that's nice!

3 tbsp. butter
2 rice-cooker cups (12 oz.) uncooked medium-grain white rice
Salt & pepper, to taste
1 (10.5-oz.) can chicken broth
6 oz. water
½ cup pecans (or your favorite nuts), chopped fine

Press down COOK switch. Add butter and melt. Add rice, salt and pepper and stir for two minutes to brown. Add remaining ingredients and cover pot. Once meal is cooked, and the COOK switch pops up to WARM mode, let it stand covered 10 minutes before serving.

Cooked for 17 minutes and made up to the 2½-cup level.

· · · · ·

"It was a very nice side dish. I served it with baked chicken and it was different than regular rice and gravy."
FLO FRITH - ABBEVILLE, LA

"Company's coming – just the thing. A great dish to accompany any entrée. We served this with spicy ribs, but it would also be delicious with beef roast, ham or turkey."
MARGARET BURLEW, EXTENSION AGENT - LSU AGCENTER - HOUMA, LA

SEAFOOD

Don't have a good local source of crawfish,
or perhaps you just don't care for crawfish?

If you like, you can substitute an equal amount of shrimp
or the fish of your choice for the crawfish in these recipes.

Catfish Sauce Piquante

Catfish cooked in tomato gravy is a Cajun/Creole classic dish.
You may substitute the fish of your choice for the catfish.

1 lb. catfish fillets, cut into bite-size pieces
2 tsp. Cajun or Creole seasoning, or to taste
TABASCO® Brand Pepper Sauce to taste, or serve at the table
1 (10-oz.) can diced tomatoes with green chilies
1 (6-oz.) can tomato paste
1 onion, chopped
1 medium bell pepper, chopped
7 cloves garlic, minced
3 green onion tops, chopped
½ to 1 stick butter, chopped
½ tsp. sugar
2 cups water
Hot, fluffy rice

Put the catfish pieces in rice cooker and season well with Cajun or Creole seasoning. Add remaining ingredients to rice cooker except rice, stir, cover and press down COOK switch. Once meal is cooked, and the COOK switch pops up to WARM mode, let it stand covered 10 minutes before serving over hot rice.

Cooked for 32 minutes and made up to the 5-cup level. Don't let it cook longer than 40 minutes.

· · · · ·

"This recipe was delicious. For some it was a little too spicy. I would look for mild tomatoes with green chilies next time. I tried it out on my neighbor and my son."
CLAUDETTE BREAUX, TVFC
LES AMIES DE BURKWALL VFC CLUB - HOUMA, LA

Crawfish and Corn Maque Choux

Corn Maque Choux (pronounced mock-shoe) is a traditional dish of southern Louisiana. We're adding crawfish to make an excellent meal everyone is sure to love. Also try our Crawfish & Corn Maque Choux Soup in the Soups chapter.

1 (14.75-oz.) can sweet cream corn
1 (15.25-oz.) can whole kernel sweet corn, drained
1 (10-oz.) can diced tomatoes with green chilies
1 onion, chopped
1 bell pepper, chopped
1 stalk celery, chopped
4 cloves garlic, minced
1 stick butter, chopped
Salt, red and black pepper, to taste
1 lb. crawfish tails, peeled and deveined
Hot cooked rice

Spray rice pot with non-stick spray. Add all ingredients to rice cooker except rice, stir well, cover and press down COOK switch. Once meal is cooked, and the COOK switch pops up to WARM mode, let it stand covered 10 minutes before serving over hot rice.

Cooked for about 30 minutes and made up to the 5-cup level.

• • • • •

"Easy and tasty."
   MARY SAMAHA - HOMEMAKERS HOLIDAY VFC CLUB - HOUMA, LA

Crawfish and Crab Dip or "Casserole"

We brought the rice cooker to the camp and cooked for our friends. Everyone enjoyed it. By the way, use real crab if available.

1 lb. crawfish tails, peeled & deveined
1 (12-oz.) package imitation crab, chopped fine
1 stick butter, chopped
1 onion, chopped
1 jalapeno pepper, chopped
1 bell pepper, chopped
5 cloves garlic, minced
½ cup chopped onion tops
½ tsp. dried parsley flakes
TABASCO® Brand Pepper Sauce to taste, or serve at the table
1¼ cups water
1 cup processed cheese

Add all ingredients to rice cooker except cheese, stir well, cover and press down COOK switch. Once meal is cooked, and the COOK switch pops up to WARM mode, add cheese, stir and serve.

Cooked for about 30 minutes and made up to the 5-cup level.

· · · · ·

"Good flavor! We served it as a dip with corn chips at a State 4-H Agents Conference and everyone wants the recipe! It can also be served as a meal over rice or pasta."
  TINA GOEBEL - 4-H YOUTH AGENT - JEFF DAVIS PARISH, LA

"This was delicious and I loved it. It was a little too salty for me, but I will try it again with salt free butter or cheese."
  LEE SIMON - KAPLAN, LA

"This was one of the best recipes I have ever used and all who tasted it said the same. I would use this in the future as a dip. I did use real crab when I cooked the dish."
  DEE MARTIN - LES AMIES DE BURKWALL CLUB - TERREBONNE VFC

Crawfish Étouffée

Here's a classic all-time favorite of south Louisiana's Cajun Country. Crawfish étouffée (pronounced A-two-FAY) is a real treat when traveling down here and visiting our popular restaurants. Now you can enjoy it from the comfort of your home.
NOTE: SHRIMP MAY BE SUBSTITUTED FOR CRAWFISH.

1 stick butter, chopped
½ small red bell pepper, chopped
½ small green bell pepper, chopped
3 green onions, chopped
3 cloves garlic, minced
1 medium onion, chopped
¼ cup minced parsley
2 dashes (1/8 tsp.) dried bay leaf flakes
1 tbsp. Worcestershire sauce
1 lb. crawfish tails, peeled and deveined
2 (10.5-oz.) cans chicken broth
Salt and pepper, to taste
TABASCO® Brand Pepper Sauce to taste, or serve at the table
2 tbsp. flour
Hot cooked rice

Press down COOK switch. Add butter and allow to melt. Sauté the vegetables for a few minutes. Add remaining ingredients. Stir flour in a little at a time, stirring constantly, so it blends thoroughly. Cover and allow to cook for no more than 35 minutes, so you don't lose all your liquid.
Serve over hot rice.

Cooked for 35 minutes and made up to the 3-cup level.

· · · · ·

CONTRIBUTED BY **STEVEN BERTRAND - LAFAYETTE, LA**

"Excellent flavors and easy to make; served with a vegetable side dish and salad for an easy and delicious meal."
MARY SAMAHA - HOMEMAKERS HOLIDAY VFC CLUB - HOUMA, LA.

Crawfish Stew

*I grew up eating Mom's stews and gumbos cooked with roux
(pronounced roo). It has a brown color and an excellent taste.
Roux can be made on the stove with equal parts oil and all-purpose
flour, but I cheat and go the easy route and use a store-bought
roux that I have good success with.*

CAUTION: THE NATURE OF ROUX HAS A TENDENCY TO FOAM AND BOIL OVER,
SO I RECOMMEND WATCHING THE POT, BEING READY TO RAISE THE
LID TO LET THE BOILING WATER SETTLE DOWN. THE TONY CHACHERE'S
(PRONOUNCED SASH-EREE) ROUX MIX LISTED BELOW HAS NOT
GIVEN ME A PROBLEM WITH BOILING OVER IN MY RICE COOKER.

NOTE: SHRIMP, FISH OR CHICKEN CUT IN BITE-SIZE PIECES
MAY BE SUBSTITUTED IN PLACE OF CRAWFISH

1 lb. peeled crawfish tails
1 tsp. Cajun or Creole seasoning
1 stick butter, chopped
1 onion, chopped
½ bell pepper, chopped
2 cloves garlic, minced
2 green onions, chopped
1 tbsp. Worcestershire sauce
TABASCO® Brand Pepper Sauce to taste, or serve at the table
¼ cup Tony Chachere's Roux Mix dissolved in 2 cups water
    in a pot on stove
1 extra cup water
Hot cooked rice

Put the crawfish tails in rice cooker and season well.
Add next seven ingredients.

To Prepare Roux Mix: In a saucepan over medium heat, whisk one-fourth
cup Roux Mix into two cups cool water. Bring to a boil, whisking until well
dissolved. After mixture begins to thicken, remove from heat, and pour into
rice cooker. Add one extra cup of water, stir well, cover and press down
COOK switch. Cook for 25-30 minutes, then lift the COOK switch up to
stop the cooking process and put in WARM mode.

Serve over hot cooked rice.
Cook for only 25 to 30 minutes; it made up to the 4-cup level.

• • • • •

"My husband loved it. This is so easy!"
MARY SAMAHA -HOMEMAKERS HOLIDAY VFC CLUB - HOUMA, LA

Smothered Crawfish

This delicious meal is waiting to be cooked. Feel free to substitute cream of mushroom soup instead of cream of celery, and add more salt and pepper if you wish. You may also substitute shrimp, fish or chicken for the crawfish.

2 sticks butter, chopped
1 lb. peeled crawfish tails, seasoned
½ tsp. Cajun or Creole seasoning
TABASCO® Brand Pepper Sauce to taste, or serve at the table
1/8 tsp. salt
1 (10.5-oz.) can cream of celery soup
1 small onion, chopped
½ large bell pepper, chopped
3 cloves garlic, minced
2 green onions, chopped
Chopped parsley, to taste
Hot cooked rice or pasta

Add all ingredients to rice cooker except rice or pasta, stir, cover and press down COOK switch. Once meal is cooked, and the COOK switch pops up to WARM mode, serve immediately over hot rice or pasta.

Cooked for 19 minutes and made up to the 3-cup level.

• • • • •

"Delicious and simple to prepare. I seasoned the crawfish with Creole seasoning and did not add additional seasoning. Used margarine instead of butter, roasted garlic cream of mushroom soup instead of cream of celery, and used one package frozen seasoning blend instead of fresh onion, bell pepper and garlic. Would like it a bit thicker, so next time I'll try mixing 3 tbsp. cornstarch in half cup of water and adding it like I do when I make étouffée. This is very similar to an étouffée. Everyone loved it! Will definitely make it again! I used a 16-cup, non-stick finish rice cooker."
PATTY VIDRINE-DAIGLE, HOME ECONOMIST
LSU AGCENTER - JEFF DAVIS PARISH, LA

SOUPS

Black-eyed Pea and Sausage Soup

I never thought you could make soup or gumbo in a rice cooker. Who would've ever thought that? But we experimented with it and came up with a real winner! Enjoy!

1 lb. smoked sausage, cut in small pieces
    and browned in skillet
3 strips bacon, cut into 1-inch pieces and cooked in skillet
2 (15.5-oz.) cans black-eyed peas with jalapenos, undrained
1 (10.5-oz.) can chicken broth
1 medium onion, chopped
3 green onions, chopped
½ cup (1 stalk) chopped celery
½ tsp. garlic powder
½ tsp. oregano
TABASCO® Brand Pepper Sauce to taste, or serve at the table
2 cups water

Drain grease from sausage and bacon; put in rice cooker.
Add remaining ingredients, stir, cover and press down COOK switch.
Allow to cook for 45 minutes, and then serve.

Made up to the 8-cup level. For a lesser amount of soup, cut the quantity of sausage, peas, chicken broth and water in half.

CONTRIBUTED BY **STEVEN BERTRAND - LAFAYETTE, LA**

• • • • •

Chicken Noodle Soup

Here's a traditional homemade soup that is tasty and hearty.

1 lb. chicken breast, or your favorite cut of chicken
1 (10.5-oz.) can cream of chicken soup
2 (10.5-oz.) cans chicken broth
1 cup baby carrots, coarsely chopped
1 rib celery, chopped
1 small onion, chopped
3 cloves garlic, minced
¼ cup chopped green onion
¼ cup parsley
6 oz. (half of a 12-oz. box) fettuccine noodles, broken in half
½ stick butter, chopped
¼ tsp. Cajun seasoning
4 cups water

Cut fat off chicken, cut in small pieces and brown in rice cooker or skillet. Add all ingredients to rice cooker, stir, cover and press down COOK switch. Allow to cook for about 45-50 minutes and serve.

Made up to the 5-cup level.

CONTRIBUTED BY **STEVEN BERTRAND - LAFAYETTE, LA**

· · · · ·

"It tastes good. I would use a little less of the noodles. Most people would probably like more seasoning."
LINDA CROCHET - JENNINGS, LA

"Delicious classic! It made my insides feel good. A great comfort food."
TOOTSIE BURLEW - HOUMA, LA

Chicken and Sausage Gumbo

Here's a classic Cajun/Creole dish that you can easily make at home. My son, Steven, has been cooking his gumbo recipe since he was nine years old. This is his basic recipe for use in your rice cooker.

1 lb. smoked sausage, cut in small pieces
1½ lbs. boneless chicken breast (or your favorite parts)
    cut in bite-size pieces
½ large (2/3 cup) bell pepper, chopped
1 small onion, chopped
3 cloves garlic, minced
1 green onion, chopped
½ tsp. salt
1 tsp. Cajun or Creole seasoning
TABASCO® Brand Pepper Sauce to taste, or serve at the table
½ cup Tony Chachere's Creole Instant Roux Mix
7 cups water, divided
Hot, fluffy rice

Brown the sausage and chicken in a skillet until done; drain any fat. Add chicken, vegetables and seasoning to rice cooker.

To Prepare Roux Mix: In a saucepan over medium heat, whisk one-half cup Roux Mix into two cups cool water. Bring to a boil, whisking until well dissolved. After mixture begins to thicken, remove from heat, and pour into rice cooker.

Add remaining five cups water to rice cooker, stir well, cover, and press down COOK switch. Allow to cook for at least 35 minutes, then turn rice cooker to WARM mode.

Serve over hot, fluffy rice.

NOTE: ROUX WILL NORMALLY CREATE FOAM AND TEND TO BOIL OVER, WHICH MEANS YOU HAVE TO WATCH THE RICE POT. I USE THIS BRAND BECAUSE IT MAKES LESS FOAM AND DID NOT BOIL OVER FOR US. BUT I DO RECOMMEND THAT YOU WATCH YOUR RICE COOKER WHILE IT IS BOILING TO BE PREPARED TO LIFT THE LID TO PREVENT A BOIL-OVER.

Cook time is 35 to 45 minutes. Makes up to 5-cup level.

CONTRIBUTED BY **STEVEN BERTRAND - LAFAYETTE, LA**

• • • • •

"I tried the Chicken and Sausage Gumbo in the rice cooker. I already use the instant roux mix, so this gumbo tastes very much like the gumbo my family loves on a cool night. Good thing I have two rice cookers, one for rice and one for the gumbo!"

MONICA OLINDE, FAMILY AND CONSUMER SCIENCES AGENT
LSU AGCENTER
POINTE COUPEE PARISH - NEW ROADS, LA

Corn and Potato Soup

Smooth and warm … Comfort food at its best!

2 (10.75-oz.) cans condensed cream of potato soup
1 (14.75-oz.) can cream style corn*
2 green onions, chopped
3 cloves garlic, minced
4 tbsp. butter
3 oz. cream cheese, room temperature, cubed
½ tsp. onion powder, or to taste
¼ tsp. black pepper, or to taste
TABASCO® Brand Pepper Sauce to taste, or serve at the table
¾ cup water
1 pint (16 oz.) half & half (light cream) or milk
Bacon bits

Add all ingredients to rice cooker except half & half and bacon bits, stir, cover and press down COOK switch. Allow to cook 30 minutes, then remove cover, add the half & half or milk, and stir. Cover and continue cooking for 10 minutes, then serve. Add bacon bits to bowl of soup.

*Note: For a less sweet-tasting soup, use fresh or frozen whole kernel corn, thawed. Perhaps canned whole kernel corn will not be as sweet.

Made up to the 5-cup level.

CONTRIBUTED BY **STEVEN BERTRAND - LAFAYETTE, LA**

• • • • •

"Very good taste. I used 'no salt added' cream style corn and it was salty enough. Would also be good with added meat like ham, cooked chicken, or seafood."
   JULIA MILLER - LAKE ARTHUR, LA

"It was very good and rich. My family loved it and I would make no changes."
   VIRGIE FOREMAN - MAURICE, LA

"I loved this soup. It was so different. I will definitely fix it again and it was easy to make in my rice cooker."
   LEE SIMON - KAPLAN, LA

Crawfish and Corn Maque Choux Soup

This is exactly the same as Crawfish & Corn Maque Choux, (pronounced "mock-shoe") except the corn is not drained, no rice is needed and half & half is added for a soup-like consistency.

1 (14.75-oz.) can sweet cream corn
1 (15.25-oz.) can whole kernel sweet corn, undrained
1 (10-oz.) can diced tomatoes with green chilies
1 onion, chopped
1 bell pepper, chopped
1 stalk celery, chopped
4 cloves garlic, minced
1 stick butter, chopped
½ tsp. Cajun or Creole seasoning
1 lb. crawfish tails, peeled and deveined
1 pint (2 cups) half & half (light cream)

Add all ingredients to rice cooker, stir, cover and press down COOK switch. Once meal is cooked, and the COOK switch pops up to WARM mode, add the half & half, stir, cover and let it stand heating 10 minutes before serving.

Took 43 minutes to cook and made up to the 7-cup level.

THANKS TO LISA LANZA-MENARD FOR THE IDEA FOR THIS SOUP.

• • • • •

"I made a few substitutions when I cooked this recipe. I used shrimp instead of crawfish, used ½ stick of light margarine, and fat-free half & half. It was awesome! I will definitely cook this recipe again."
LETHA VINCENT - CROWLEY, LA

"I tried this soup with shrimp because I did not have fresh Louisiana crawfish and we liked it. I will try this with crawfish later on when they are in season. I floated a few onion tops on top when I served it."
FLO FRITH - ABBEVILLE, LA

"This recipe was very tasty, but I found it too spicy. My husband, on the other hand, who was brought up in the Atchafalaya Basin, thought it was good as is. The use of a can of mild diced tomatoes with green chilies would help for my taste buds. Cooking in my rice cooker was longer than the 43 minutes stated in the recipe."
BETTY GUILBEAU, TVFC - LES AMIES DE BURKWALL VFC CLUB - HOUMA, LA

Steak and Potato Soup

This is basically the same recipe as the Cajun Pepper Steak found in the Meats chapter, but with a few added ingredients to make a very hearty and filling soup.

1 lb. boneless round steak,
    cut into very small pieces and seasoned
½ tsp. Cajun or Creole seasoning
Salt, to taste
1 tbsp. butter
½ large onion, chopped
½ bell pepper, chopped
5 garlic cloves, minced
1 (.87-oz.) envelope Brown Gravy Mix
4 medium potatoes, (4 cups), peeled and cubed
1 (10.75-oz.) can cream of potato soup
1 (10.5-oz.) can beef broth
1 (10-oz.) can diced tomatoes with green chilies
2 tsp. Worcestershire sauce
1/8 tsp. dried bay leaf flakes
½ tsp. dried basil
1 pint half and half
TABASCO® Brand Pepper Sauce to taste, or serve at the table
Shredded mild cheddar cheese, as garnish
½ cup finely chopped green onion, as garnish
½ cup finely chopped parsley, as garnish
Sour cream, as garnish (optional)

Add the seasoned meat, butter, onion, bell pepper and garlic to rice cooker, cover and press COOK switch; cook for about 10 minutes; keep the gravy. Add Brown Gravy Mix packet to a bowl with one cup cold water, stir to dissolve well. Add to rice cooker. Add remaining ingredients to rice cooker except garnish items, then stir and cover. Cook for about 50 minutes until potatoes are tender, and then serve immediately.

Cook soup for only 50 minutes. It made up to the 8-cup level.

NOTE: MAKE THIS SOUP SOUTHWESTERN-STYLE BY ADDING ONE-HALF TO ONE CAN OF
       BOTH BLACK BEANS AND WHOLE KERNEL CORN, DRAINED, AND ONE-HALF TO
       ONE TEASPOON CUMIN. GARNISH AS SUGGESTED ABOVE, WITH THE ADDITION
       OF AVOCADO SLICES (OPTIONAL) AND/OR SOUR CREAM.

CONTRIBUTED BY LISA MENARD - LAFAYETTE, LA

Taco Soup

What great Mexican flavors!
Feel free to increase the seasoning level if you wish.

1 lb. ground meat, browned
Salt and pepper, to taste
½ tsp. chili powder
½ tsp. garlic powder
½ tsp. onion powder
1 (15.25-oz.) can whole kernel corn, undrained
1 (15.5-oz.) can chili beans with liquid
1 (10-oz.) can diced tomatoes with green chilies, undrained
1 medium onion, chopped
4 cups tomato juice
1 (1.5-oz.) envelope taco seasoning
1 cup water

Drain meat of any grease; add to rice cooker with remaining ingredients, stir, cover and press down COOK switch. Cook soup for 45 minutes then stop. Serve hot.

Cook for 45 minutes; it made up to the 7-cup level.

· · · · ·

"We really enjoyed this soup. I will definitely make this again (especially in the winter time). We ate it with corn chips but want to try it with tortilla chips or cornbread."
PEGGY GISCLAIR - VERMILION PARISH, LA

"¡Olé! This one is a "keeper". We added corn chips and a little cheese to complete this great taste. And so easy to prepare."
MARGARET & TOOTSIE BURLEW - HOUMA, LA

VEGETABLES
POTATOES, CABBAGE & SWEET POTATOES

Chicken Fajita Stuffed Potato

I love stuffed, baked potatoes! My son Steven and I had fun coming up with these two tasty stuffed potato recipes. And as a bonus, here's a time-saving shortcut. By using the frozen, crinkle-cut, French-fried potatoes, you eliminate the peeling and cutting of potatoes!

1 lb. boneless, skinless chicken breast cut in thin strips
Salt, red & black pepper, to taste
1 (1.12-oz.) envelope chicken fajita mix
1 (2-lb.) bag frozen, crinkle-cut French-fried potatoes, defrosted
1 medium onion cut in thin strips
½ red bell pepper cut in thin strips
1 stick butter, chopped
1 (10.5-oz.) can chicken broth
6 oz. water
TABASCO® Brand Pepper Sauce to taste, or serve at the table

Brown chicken in skillet on stove, and drain excess grease. Season chicken with salt and peppers and stir. Dissolve fajita mix in bowl according to package directions. Add all ingredients to rice cooker, stir, cover and press down COOK switch. Once meal is cooked, and the COOK switch pops up to WARM mode, let it stand covered 10 minutes before serving.

Cooked for 41 minutes and made up to the 5-cup level.

CONTRIBUTED BY **NEAL & STEVEN BERTRAND - LAFAYETTE, LA**

• • • • •

"Enjoyed by family gathering which had pork and sausage jambalaya as the main dish. However, everyone wanted to know about this tasty side dish. Indeed it was very flavorful and all wanted to take home a copy of the recipe. It was very easy to prepare and I would recommend it as a quick and easy dish for any occasion. Several in the family want a copy of the rice cooker cookbook when it comes out."
PEGGY GARY - JENNINGS VFC - JENNINGS, LA

"This was a really good tasting stuffed potato. After dishing it into a bowl I sprinkled it with a little shredded cheese."
FLO FRITH - ABBEVILLE, LA

Chili and Cheese Stuffed Potato

This is an All-American meal, hearty enough for even the biggest appetites. A major crowd pleaser!

1 lb. ground beef or turkey, browned, drained
Salt, red & black pepper, to taste
1 tsp. chili powder
1 (1.25-oz.) envelope chili seasoning mix
1 (2-lb.) bag frozen, crinkle-cut
    French-fried potatoes, defrosted
1 (15.5-oz.) can small red beans in
    spicy tomato sauce (Chili Beans)
1 stick butter, chopped
1 medium onion, chopped
1 (8-oz.) can tomato sauce
1 ½ cups water
TABASCO® Brand Pepper Sauce to taste or serve at the table
1 (8-oz.) package shredded Monterey Jack
    or your favorite cheese
Sour cream (optional)
Chopped green onion tops (optional)

Place ground meat in rice cooker, season well with salt, pepper, chili powder, chili seasoning mix and stir. Add remaining ingredients to rice cooker except cheese, sour cream and onion tops. Stir and mix well, pressing down on the potatoes to coat with liquid. Cover and press down COOK switch. Once meal is cooked, and the COOK switch pops up to WARM mode, remove lid and stir well, which will break up the remaining unbroken potatoes. Place a serving on plate and add cheese and mix well. Add sour cream, onion tops or any of the traditional baked potato fixings.

Cooked for 25 minutes and made up to the 8-cup level.

CONTRIBUTED BY **NEAL & STEVEN BERTRAND - LAFAYETTE, LA**

• • • • •

"I shared this dish with friends and they all enjoyed it. Be careful with seasoning. The envelope of chili seasoning mix I used was very peppery and you really had to enjoy extremely spicy food to like this dish. Since it called for chili powder, chili seasoning mix and salt, red, and black pepper you might caution people about the seasoning."
DEE MARTIN - LES AMIES DE BURKWALL CLUB - TERREBONNE VFC

"Crawfish Boil" Potatoes

When we have our family crawfish boil, we always put potatoes and corn-on-the-cob into the pot along with the crawfish. I had the idea of doing the same thing in a rice pot. It came out great the first time we tried it. You may want to experiment with some small corn-on-the-cob pieces, putting them in with the potatoes, or by putting them in the steamer basket of your rice cooker, if you have one.

2 cups water
1 tsp. liquid crab & shrimp boil
1 tsp. salt
½ tsp. red pepper
1 stick butter, chopped
3 lbs. red potatoes, cleaned well, unpeeled,
    diced into 1-inch pieces
1 large onion, chopped fine

Add all ingredients to rice cooker in order above, stir, cover and press down COOK switch. Once meal is cooked, and the COOK switch pops up to WARM mode, let it stand covered 10 minutes before serving.

Cook time is about one hour. Makes up to the 5-cup level.

· · · · ·

"I made the crawfish boiled potatoes in my rice cooker. The next time I cook it I'll decrease the amount of salt a bit."
    STEVE BOREL, ASSOCIATE COUNTY AGENT
    POINTE COUPEE PARISH - NEW ROADS, LA

Easy Smothered Potatoes and Sausage

This savory meal goes well as a side or main dish.
And it's fast, using the frozen potatoes shortcut.

3 links (1 lb.) smoked sausage, cut in small pieces
1 (2-lb.) bag frozen, crinkle-cut French-fried potatoes, defrosted
1 (1-oz.) package onion soup mix, dissolved in 2 cups water
1 onion, chopped
4 cloves garlic, minced
Salt, red & black pepper, to taste
1 stick butter, chopped

Brown sausage in skillet on stove or rice cooker, drain excess grease. Add all ingredients to rice cooker, stir, cover and press down COOK switch. Once meal is cooked, and the COOK switch pops up to WARM mode, let it stand covered 10 minutes before serving.

Cooked for 30 minutes and made up to the 5-cup level.

• • • • •

"Fantastic – emptied the pot! Everybody loved it! I substituted onion soup mix with mushrooms for the plain onion soup mix."
DOT HARPER - WELSH VFC - WELSH, LA

"Great, tasty, and fast recipe! The use of the already cut French-fried potatoes lessens the preparation time greatly. Cooked in 30 minutes as stated in the recipe."
BETTY GUILBEAU, TVFC - LES AMIES DE BURKWALL VFC CLUB - HOUMA, LA

Sausage, Potatoes and Green Beans

Supper's done! All in one rice pot! Call the kids! The whole family will enjoy this hearty and very tasty meal.

1 lb. smoked sausage, sliced small and browned, drained
2 lbs. (about 5 medium) potatoes, cleaned well,
    unpeeled and diced
1 (14.5-oz.) can green beans with liquid
1 (10.5-oz.) can beef broth
1 medium onion, chopped
½ bell pepper, chopped
½ stick butter, chopped
Salt and pepper, to taste
Onion and garlic powder, to taste
1 cup water

Add all ingredients to rice cooker, stir, cover and press down COOK switch. Once meal is cooked, and the COOK switch pops up to WARM mode, remove cover, stir and serve hot.

Turned cooker off after 1 hour 10 minutes, and it made up to the 5-cup level. You may want to test for potato tenderness after 50 to 60 minutes.

· · · · ·

Smothered Potatoes
with Sausage and Tasso

Thanks to Sandra Degeytaire of M&S Grocery for contributing the idea for this recipe. This is one of the side dishes served with their popular plate lunches (except they do not put tasso in theirs); and thanks to Romona Ortego at Floyd's Wholesale for the idea of adding tasso to this dish.

NOTE: FOR A SPICIER DISH, USE A "HOT" SAUSAGE INSTEAD OF "MILD."

What is tasso? Tasso is a south Louisiana specialty meat product made from the pork shoulder. It is typically fatty with a lot of flavor. It's cut into three or four-inch pieces, briefly soaked in a salt mixture, and left to cure three or four hours. It is then rinsed, rubbed with a spice mixture containing cayenne pepper, garlic, and other seasonings, and hot-smoked until cooked through. It is not eaten on its own, but used to enhance the flavor of meals.

1 lb. smoked link sausage,
**   sliced into bite-size pieces and browned**
½ lb. (8 oz.) smoked pork tasso, diced and browned
2 lbs. white or red potatoes, peeled and diced
7 cloves garlic, chopped, or to taste
1 small onion, chopped
1 tsp. Cajun or Creole seasoning
1 stick butter, chopped
1 (1-oz.) envelope onion soup mix
2 cups (16 oz.) water

Add all ingredients to rice cooker, stir, cover and press down COOK switch. Once meal is cooked, and the COOK switch pops up to WARM mode, uncover, stir well, and serve hot.

Cooked for 52 minutes and made up to the 6-cup level.

· · · · ·

Turkey and Potatoes in Barbecue Sauce

Ground turkey...potatoes...your favorite barbecue sauce.
Yum! This is so good! Try it.

1 lb. ground turkey or beef, browned, drained
Salt and pepper, to taste
1 tsp. chili powder
1 tsp. garlic powder
TABASCO® Brand Pepper Sauce to taste, or serve at the table
Barbecue seasoning, to taste
2 lbs. (about 5 medium) potatoes, cleaned,
    unpeeled and diced
1 medium onion, chopped
½ cup chopped green onion
¼ cup parsley
2 cups (16-oz.) jar barbecue sauce
2¼ cups water

Place drained meat with all ingredients in rice cooker, stir, cover and press down COOK switch. Once meal is cooked, and the COOK switch pops up to WARM mode, uncover, stir and serve.

Cooked for about 40 minutes and made up to the 6-cup level.

· · · · ·

Cabbage "Casserole" I

Cabbage in a rice cooker is a very popular dish and goes by various names, such as Almost Cabbage Rolls. It's all good. We got lots of compliments on it.

1 lb. ground meat
1 lb. smoked sausage, sliced
1 medium onion, chopped
1 medium bell pepper, chopped
4-5 green onions, chopped
Chopped parsley, optional
Salt and pepper, to taste
Garlic powder, to taste
TABASCO® Brand Pepper Sauce to taste, or serve at the table
1 (10-oz.) can of diced tomatoes with green chilies, undrained
1 cup water
1 cup (8 oz.) uncooked medium-grain white rice
1 small head of cabbage, chopped

Press down COOK switch. Spray bottom of pot with non-stick vegetable spray. Add ground meat, sausage and chopped vegetables, except cabbage. Cover and allow to cook for about 10 minutes.

Remove lid and continue to cook ingredients, browning the ground meat and sausage, and sautéing the vegetables. Add seasonings, and then stir. Continue to cook until the meat is browned and the vegetables are cooked down. Add diced tomatoes, water, rice, and then stir and add cabbage.

Cover and cook until the meal is cooked and the COOK switch pops up to WARM mode. Let it stand, covered, for 10 minutes before serving. Remove lid. Stir all ingredients together and serve.

Serves 4 to 8 people, depending on if this dish is being used as a main dish or a side dish.

Recommended for an 8-cup rice cooker.

CONTRIBUTED BY **BELINDA SAVOIE - CROWLEY, LA**

· · · · ·

"I really enjoyed this cabbage casserole. I had never tried browning
ground meat in the rice cooker before. I didn't know it could be done.
I drained the meat mixture before adding Rotel, water, and rice."

MILES BRASHIER, COUNTY AGENT
POINTE COUPEE PARISH
NEW ROADS, LA

"One son-in-law loved it and the other one did not. The rest
of the family loved it. It was delicious and eye appealing."

VIRGIE FOREMAN
MAURICE, LA

"When I read this recipe, I thought it sounded strange with the smoked sausage in it as I
don't cook smoked sausage and cabbage together. The combination was OK. I enjoyed it."

MARY HILL
LES AMIES DE BURKWALL
TERREBONNE VFC

Cabbage "Casserole" II

Cooked cabbage was never a favorite of mine growing up, but these two contributed cabbage recipes made a believer out of me. Wow! So good!

½ lb. ground beef, browned
½ lb. smoked sausage, sliced and browned
6 cups (12 oz. by weight) of shredded cabbage
1 (10-oz.) can diced tomatoes with green chilies
1 (10.5-oz.) can beef broth
1 stick butter
1½ rice cooker cups (8 oz.) uncooked medium-grain white rice
1 cup chopped onion
¾ cup chopped bell pepper
½ tsp. garlic powder
Salt and pepper, to taste
TABASCO® Brand Pepper Sauce to taste, or serve at the table
1½ cups water

Add all ingredients to rice cooker, stir, cover and press down COOK switch. Once meal is cooked, and the COOK switch pops up to WARM mode, let it stand covered 10 minutes before serving.

Cooked for 36 minutes and made up to the 7-cup level.

CONTRIBUTED BY **ELSIE CASTILLE, FCE VOLUNTEER - BREAUX BRIDGE, LA**

· · · · ·

"I added the onions and bell peppers to the ground meat and sausage and sautéed them together. I used smoked turkey sausage and lean ground beef to make it healthier, and it tasted great! Super good!"
LETHA VINCENT - CROWLEY, LA

"I love cooked cabbage. This is an easy way to use cabbage instead of making cabbage rolls. It cuts your work in half and just as good."
MARY SAMAHA - HOMEMAKERS HOLIDAY VFC CLUB - HOUMA, LA

Candied Yams with Marshmallows

Mom and Dad made candied yams every year for our Thanksgiving family get-togethers. They cooked them in the oven. They always made them the day before and left them on the table overnight, covered, during which time the thin syrup thickened. I remember it took them several hours to get a finished product. I converted their recipe to be cooked in a rice cooker, and it cooked for one hour. What a time-saver and just as tasty!

2¼ pounds raw yams (sweet potatoes),
    peeled & diced into small cubes
½ stick butter, chopped
½ bottle (8 oz.) light corn syrup
1 (5-oz.) can evaporated milk
Juice of 1 lemon
½ tsp. cinnamon
Pinch of nutmeg
1 cup (8 oz.) water
2 cups large marshmallows, or to taste
1 cup chopped pecans

Add all ingredients to rice cooker except marshmallows and pecans, stir, cover and press down COOK switch. Once yams are cooked, and the COOK switch pops up to WARM mode, add marshmallows and pecans and stir. Cover and let it stand covered 10 minutes before serving.

Cooked for 56 minutes and made up to the 4-cup level.

· · · · ·

"Very good. Liked the flavor better when it had cooled down a bit.
Was really curious how this would turn out, and it was a success!"
    DOT MELANCON DAIGLE - JENNINGS VFC - JENNINGS, LA

"I made the candied yams recipe in the rice cooker. I love them."
    STEVE BOREL, ASSOCIATE COUNTY AGENT
    POINTE COUPEE PARISH - NEW ROADS, LA

"This was a good recipe. Since I am a diabetic using the white corn syrup and no sugar is good for me. After I took it out of the rice cooker, I put the yams in individual servings in small custard cups and it was very attractive."
    VIRGIE FOREMAN - MAURICE, LA

"This was easy and very good. I only had to purchase the yams.
I had everything else in my kitchen."
    MARY HILL - LES AMIES DE BURKWALL - TERREBONNE VFC

Yams with Brown Sugar and Butter

This is a delicious dish. The yams turned out very soft and made a brown syrup liquid which candied after refrigerating.

1¼ lbs. uncooked yams, peeled and diced in half-inch cubes
½ cup brown sugar, packed
½ stick butter, chopped
1½ cups water

Add all ingredients to rice cooker, stir, cover and press down COOK switch. Once yams are cooked, and the COOK switch pops up to WARM mode, let it stand covered 10 minutes before serving.

Cooked for 46 minutes and made up to the 2.5-cup level.

• • • • •

"I used 1/3 cup Splenda® Brown Sugar instead of regular brown sugar. Great tasting recipe!"
   LETHA VINCENT - CROWLEY, LA

"This came out very good. We all loved it!"
   JOY BISSEN - DE SOTO, WI

RESOURCES

THE WELL-STOCKED RICE COOKER MEALS PANTRY

These ingredients appear in the pages of this cookbook and are listed here as a convenient shopping list.

MEATS & SEAFOOD

Bacon
Beef roast
Catfish fillets
Chicken
Crabmeat
Crawfish tails
Frozen cooked meatballs
Ground meat: beef, pork, turkey, etc.
Pepperoni slices
Round steak
Shrimp
Smoked pork Tasso
Smoked Sausage: beef,
  pork or turkey

CANNED VEGETABLES, BROTH, ETC.

Beans, chili
Beans, green
Beans, red
Beans, red chili beans in spicy
  tomato sauce
Black-eyed peas with jalapenos
Broth, beef
Broth, chicken
Corn, cream style
Corn, whole kernel
Evaporated milk
Mushrooms
Rotel (diced tomatoes
  with green chilies)
Soup, cream of celery
Soup, cream of chicken
Soup, cream of potato
Tomato paste
Tomato sauce

RICE & POTATOES

Medium or long grain white rice
Frozen crinkle-cut
  French-fried potatoes
Red or white potatoes

PRODUCE

Baby Carrots
Bell pepper, green
Bell pepper, red
Black olives
Cabbage
Celery
Chopped green chilies
Eggplant
Frozen sweet peas
Garlic
Green onions
Jalapeno peppers
Lemon
Onion, purple
Onion, white or yellow
Parsley
Sweet potatoes/Yams
Zucchini

SEASONING

Bacon bits
Barbecue seasoning
Basil
Bay leaf flakes
Black pepper
Cajun or Creole seasoning
Chili powder
Cinnamon
Cumin

Dried parsley flakes
Garlic powder
Ginger root
Italian seasonings
Lemon pepper
Liquid Crab or Shrimp Boil
Nutmeg
Onion powder
Onion Soup Mix
Oregano
Red pepper
Salt
Seasoning blend
Seasoning mix, Chicken Fajita
Seasoning mix, Chili
Seasoning mix, Taco
Sugar
Sugar, brown
Tabasco® Sauce
Turmeric

PASTA
Egg noodles
Elbow macaroni
Fettuccine noodles
Spaghetti

CHEESE
Colby/Monterey Jack cheese
Mexican-style shredded cheese
Parmesan cheese
Salsa Con Queso cheese dip
Shredded Mozzarella cheese
Shredded sharp cheddar cheese
Velveeta processed cheese

SAUCES & GRAVY
Alfredo sauce
Barbecue sauce
Brown gravy mix
Enchilada sauce
Pizza sauce
Soy sauce
Spaghetti sauce
Tony Chachere's Roux Mix
Worcestershire sauce

MISCELLANEOUS
Butter
Chopped pecans or nuts
Cola
Chips, corn
Chips, Nacho cheese
Cream cheese
Eggs
Flour
Half & Half cream
Light corn syrup
Marshmallows
Non-stick vegetable spray
Olive oil
Pimento
Raisins
Shredded coconut flakes
Sour cream
Tomato juice

SAFETY PRECAUTION

Be aware that when the cooker is cooking your meal,
there is a steam vent in the lid spewing out very hot steam
that can hurt an unwary cook. I know from experience.
I got burned once when I was talking to friends and not
paying attention to what I was doing. Always be conscious
of where the vent is and position it away from where
you will grab the handle to remove the lid.

Otherwise, if you cannot trust yourself to remember that,
please use an oven mitt or kitchen towel to lift the lid.

BOILING POINT AND ALTITUDE

Altitude affects the temperature at which water boils and thus the
cooking time. It's especially true at high altitudes where longer cooking
times are necessary. At sea level the boiling point of water is 212 degrees F
(100 degrees C.). The boiling point of a liquid is lowered if the pressure of
the surrounding gases is decreased. For example, on top of Mount Everest
water will boil at 156.2 degrees F (69 degrees C). All of the meals in
this cookbook have been cooked in my rice cooker at an altitude
of 36 feet above sea level, which is the altitude of my beautiful city,
Lafayette, Louisiana. Having said all this, please take into consideration
how your altitude will affect the length of cooking time for these meals.

EASY COOKING, GREAT EATING FOR COLLEGE STUDENTS

Students! Why live on junk food when you can have food that's good for you? Are you living away from home in the dorm or off-campus, away from Mom's good cooking? You can cook nourishing, delicious, home-cooked meals in a rice cooker.

Most of these recipes are simple enough to prepare and have an average cooking time of just 30 minutes.

You live in a dorm, and you don't have a kitchen to chop vegetables. **PROBLEM?** *Maybe not.* You can just as easily substitute pre-chopped vegetables in any recipe, found in your local grocer's frozen or seafood section.

NOW YOU CAN COOK OUTSIDE!

Attention, outdoor and camping enthusiasts! You will appreciate the ease and convenience of being able to cook a meal on the road in your rice cooker. All you need is a power inverter.

Power inverters convert a 12 volt DC (car battery) power into 120V AC household electrical power. This will allow you to power your rice cooker and other equipment you use at home while camping, or when you go to the big game and have a tailgate party... or wherever. Whether you have a car, truck, RV, or boat, you can have a hot, home-cooked meal using your rice cooker.

WHAT KIND OF POWER INVERTER DO YOU NEED?

You must get a power inverter that will be sufficient to provide for your needs. If you want to run a 700-watt rice cooker, a 500-watt inverter *will not* work. You'll probably blow a fuse. Add up the wattage of all the items you plan to run through your inverter, and then get one that can handle the load.

Power inverters are available at electronics stores or online.

BROWNING MEAT: IN A SKILLET OR IN THE RICE COOKER?

Most people are amazed to learn that meat can be browned in a rice cooker. Yes, it is true; meat *can* be browned in a rice cooker. I do it all the time.

Personally, I like to brown the meat because I like the flavor better.

You have a choice of browning the meat in your rice cooker or in a skillet on the stove. Either one is fine. There is a pro and con for either method.

BROWNING IN THE RICE COOKER

THE CON: Some meat is drier and produces less gravy than others, like chicken; therefore the cooker tends to flip to WARM prematurely before the meat is browned. Simply unplug it, add a little water or broth to the pot, wait a few minutes, re-plug and it will keep cooking.

NOTE: If you lift the pot out of the rice cooker it will automatically flip to WARM. It could be a little difficult to drain the extra grease from the meat you are browning without the rice cooker flipping to warm. The only way to do it is to grab the pot and cooker with one hand using a pot holder (so you don't burn yourself) and carefully tip it to one side while draining the excess liquid with a spoon.

THE PRO: *If you choose to brown the meat in the rice cooker, you won't have a skillet to clean.*

BROWNING IN THE SKILLET

THE PRO: If you decide to brown the meat in a skillet on the stove, you can be chopping vegetables or getting something else prepped at the same time, and not be concerned the cooker will flip to WARM prematurely. Also, it is easier to remove the extra grease from the skillet with a spoon. Personally, this is my preferred method, especially if you have over a pound of meat to brown.

THE CON: *Cleaning the skillet.*

BROWNING GROUND MEAT

It is for safety reasons that the Extension Home Economists at Louisiana State University (LSU) AgCenter and I recommend browning ground meat. This way you are certain the meat is cooked thoroughly. However, if you choose not to brown the meat in a skillet, you can just put the ground meat in the rice cooker and it will get hot enough to cook it thoroughly.

HOW TO COOK WHITE RICE AND BROWN RICE IN YOUR RICE COOKER

NOTE: In all rice recipes, notice if we call for a "rice-cooker cup" (which is ¾ of a standard measuring cup) or a "standard measuring cup" (which is 8 ounces, or 1 cup).

TO COOK WHITE RICE

Use the rice cooker cup that came with the cooker and measure the amount of uncooked medium-grain white rice cups you want to cook – let's say three cups – and put rice in rice pot. Add water up to the 3-cup line, add a little salt, and press down COOK switch. If the rice cooker cup is missing, it's three-fourths of a standard measuring cup (3/4 cup).

TO COOK BROWN RICE

Add whatever quantity of brown rice you want to cook, and then just double the amount of water. For example, if you want 3 cups brown rice, add 6 cups water.

HOW YOUR RICE COOKER KNOWS WHEN THE MEAL IS COOKED

This is how the simple **COOK/WARM** rice cooker works.

If you remove the pot from the rice cooker and look inside the base you will notice the circular heating element with a round, spring tension metal device in the center of the heating plate. That is the thermostat.

At sea level, water boils at 212 degrees F/100 degrees C. While cooking, the rice (or food) and water mixture is boiling at 212 degrees.

At the end of the cooking process, when the water is both absorbed by the rice/food, and boiled off through the vent hole, the heat rises in the pot.

The thermostat is set to go off at a temperature that is higher than the boiling point of water. The thermostat senses the heat rising and switches automatically to the "Keep Warm" mode, which is approximately 150 degrees F/65 degrees C.

WANT TO COOK, BUT YOU'RE IN AN INCONVENIENT PLACE?

Are you going to a location where you want to cook a rice cooker meal, but it would not be practical to chop the ingredients? Then do what I do when I give a cooking demonstration. I chop all my vegetable ingredients the night before, and I slice the meat and brown it in a skillet. I put the ingredients in a plastic storage bag, put it in a portable cooler with ice, bring a can opener to open my canned ingredients, and I can cook anywhere there is electricity.

WHAT IF MY RICE COOKER FLIPS TO WARM PREMATURELY?

The reason your rice cooker will flip to WARM before the meal is cooked is because the temperature has risen above the boiling point, 212 degrees F.

It has happened to me when browning meat and, mistakenly allowing all the water to boil off and evaporate, thus causing the heat to rise; so the thermostat senses the temperature rising and automatically shuts off.

Unlike a skillet, a rice cooker needs liquid to operate. Don't let all the liquid boil off when browning, or cooking, meat.

Or, it could be that if you have a pot full of food, the water has evaporated at the bottom part of the pot, but still have water at the top of the pot. In this situation, just unplug it, stir well to get the water to the bottom of the pot, let it cool for a few minutes, plug in and press COOK. You're back on your way to a delicious meal.

So, if your rice cooker flips to WARM prematurely, it is sensing the food is cooked when it is not. All you need to do is to unplug the cooker, add about one-fourth cup of water or broth to your rice cooker, (depending on the situation), stir the contents and cool off the rice pot for a few minutes. Then cover, re-plug and press COOK.

TIME-SAVING TIPS
ON FOOD PREPARATION

Having a simple food processor can make chopping vegetables so much easier. Chop several onions, bell pepper, green onion, garlic, etc. at a time, put each portion in its own plastic freezer bag and put it in the freezer till needed.

Do the same for the meats. You can slice and brown sausage, ground beef, pork, turkey, or your favorite meats. Store them in the freezer. When you get home from work or school, your ingredients are prepared; just add the canned ingredients and the seasonings of your choice, and you are ready to eat in about 30 minutes.

For more thorough cooking of meats, cut your meats, chicken, etc., into very small pieces.

Butter Measurements
1 stick = 1/4 lb., 8 tbsp.; ½ cup; 4 oz.
½ stick = 4 tbsp = ¼ cup
¼ stick = 2 tbsp.

Teaching children how to cook with a rice cooker

Imagine that, teaching your children how to cook a simple meal in your rice cooker! I know that 4-H cooking clubs Junior Division starts with 4th graders, which is around 10 years old. What a beneficial life experience, to learn this skill at an early age. And what an easy way to get a Blue Ribbon First Prize with your rice cooker meal...hopefully with a recipe from this cookbook. If that happens, be sure to let Neal know about it!

STEAMING VEGETABLES IN YOUR RICE COOKER

One of the quickest and healthiest ways to cook vegetables is by steaming them in your rice cooker using the steamer basket. The vegetables retain more of their natural taste, texture, color, vitamins and minerals. Here's a brief list of fresh vegetables that can be steamed: asparagus, bean sprouts, beets, bok choy, broccoli, Brussels sprouts, cabbage, carrots, cauliflower, collared greens, corn on the cob, kale, mushrooms, onions, potatoes, spinach, squash, sweet potatoes, turnips, and zucchini.

ADD SOME FLAVOR

Steamed vegetables can tend to be a bit bland and boring, so try this. Each time you steam vegetables, be a little creative and experiment by adding a different ingredient to the water to add flavor. Here are some choices to consider, depending on your tastes and what you are steaming: lemon juice or fresh lemon, wine, soy sauce, Italian dressing, Cajun or Creole seasoning, seasoned salt, onion, garlic, barbecue sauce, or liquid crab boil.

Most important of all, please use pure, filtered water, which is the basis for a healthy lifestyle, and a stainless steel rice cooker. Stainless steel is healthier and will not release heavy metals or harmful chemicals as aluminum or non-stick coated surfaces can. If you do not have a stainless steel rice cooker, please see the rice cooker we endorse on page 94. You'll notice the steaming basket fits nicely on top of the rice cooker.

STEAMING TIMES

Put about a cup of water in the rice cooker, place the steamer basket on top with the veggies in it, cover and press COOK. Once the water starts boiling, start timing. Do not let all the water boil off. When cooking times indicated have been reached, test with a fork for desired consistency. When done, manually flip button to WARM and unplug.

The steaming times below are approximate and must be adjusted to suit your own taste, the quantity and thickness of the food.

BEAN SPROUTS, MUSHROOMS (FRESH, SLICED): 3 – 4 MINUTES

PEA PODS: 4 – 6 MINUTES

CABBAGE, SHREDDED: 6 – 8 MINUTES

COLLARED GREENS, SPINACH: 6 – 11 MINUTES

ASPARAGUS, GREEN BEANS, CARROTS: 8 – 10 MINUTES

CELERY, POTATO: 8 -12 MINUTES

ZUCCHINI: 10 -12 MINUTES

BROCCOLI, BRUSSELS SPROUTS, CAULIFLOWER: 11 – 13 MINUTES

SQUASH: 13 -16 MINUTES

FOOD AND SPICE RESOURCES

If you need ingredients that you can't find locally, contact
these reliable manufacturers through their websites listed below.

www.zatarain.com
Ready-to-serve mixes, rice dinner mixes, seafood boils, seasoning & spices,
stuffing mixes, condiments & sauces.

www.tonychachere.com
Seasoning blends, roux mix, box dinner mixes, gravy mixes, fry batters, and
marinades.

www.savoiesfoods.com
Smoked sausages, andouille sausage & boudin, smoked & seasoned meats,
dressing mix & sauces, roux, seafood pies, ready prepared entrees.

www.tabasco.com
Pepper sauces, condiments, steak sauces & marinades, chili, and snacks.

www.jackmillers.com
Barbecue and cocktail sauces and seasonings.

www.slapyamama.com
Cajun seasoning, including a white and red pepper blend; seafood boil.

INDEX OF RICE COOKER RECIPES

INDEX BY CATEGORY

REQUEST FOR RICE COOKER
RECIPES AND/OR SUGGESTIONS

1) If you or someone you know has created a rice cooker recipe that should be published, please send it to us and we'll publish it, and give proper credit for being the contributor and print their name and town under the recipe as I've done for others in this book.

2) If you have a <u>suggestion</u> for what you think will make a great recipe, send it to us as well. We'll try our best to create it, we'll publish it, and give you the credit for being the contributor and print your name and town under the recipe as I've done for others in this book.

To send a recipe or a suggestion for one, email us at **www.RiceCookerMeals.com** and click "Submit a Recipe" or mail us:

> ATTN: Recipe Dept.
> Cypress Cove Publishing
> P.O. Box 91626
> Lafayette, LA 70509-1626

. . . . .

Merchants Wanted!
Looking for a good profit? Call Neal Bertrand for discounts and details on selling our fast-moving merchandise. (337) 224-6576

Visit WWW.CYPRESSCOVEPUBLISHING.COM
See our best-selling books, beautiful Louisiana art prints, rice cookers, mouth-watering free recipes and some of the funniest family-friendly jokes you'll ever read.

ABOUT THE AUTHOR

Neal Bertrand was born and reared in Opelousas, Louisiana, in the heart of Cajun Country. He has more than a decade of experience in the publishing business. He is the founder and owner of Cypress Cove Publishing in Lafayette, Louisiana. His two previous publications are *Down-Home Cajun Cooking Favorites* and the bi-lingual (English & French) *Cajun Country Fun Coloring and Activity Book.*

He has also published a collection of authentic Cajun art prints – beautiful South Louisiana landscapes, all painted by his father, Curtis. All of his books, art prints, rice cookers and other products can be seen and ordered from his websites, **WWW.CYPRESSCOVEPUBLISHING.COM** and **WWW.RICECOOKERMEALS.COM.**

Finally, a rice cooker with a stainless steel inner bowl!

Take your *Rice Cooker Meals* cooking to a new level of health and efficiency! Introducing our incredible, new 8-cup *Miracle* brand Stainless Steel Rice Cooker and Steamer!

- Cooks your meal automatically and then switches to a "stay-warm" mode when meal is fully cooked, keeping food warm for hours.

- This 8-cup cooker will yield a full 12 cups of cooked white or brown rice.

- The inner cooking pot is a beautiful solid mirror-finish stainless steel.

- The glass lid allows you to view the rice or vegetables while cooking.

- The stainless steel steaming tray fits on top of pot so you can steam vegetables to perfection (like yummy corn-on-the-cob) while cooking your meal.

- The easy view indicator lights identify cooking and warming cycles.

- Rice measuring cup and stirring paddle included for your convenience.

- 500 watts, 120 volts, 60 Hz

$79.95 *Order yours today!*
SEE ORDER FORM

RICE COOKER MEALS:
FAST HOME COOKING FOR BUSY PEOPLE

Fast, easy meals you can cook in a rice cooker; most have a 30-minute cook time. Convenient one-pot cooking means less mess to clean, easier to have good home cooking; less expensive and healthier than "fast-food." Great for busy people, college students, tailgating parties, campers/RVers, etc. Has 60 recipes to cook delicious pastas, seafood, soups, potatoes, cabbage, sweet potatoes, jambalayas and rice side dishes. Includes Mexican, Italian, Tex-Mex and Cajun recipes. 96 PAGES, 6 X 9 SOFT COVER, $12.95

DOWN-HOME CAJUN COOKING FAVORITES

A collection of classic recipes from the south Louisiana region called Acadiana, or Cajun Country. They were contributed by area folks who are tremendous cooks in their own right, who learned how to cook these dishes passed down from generation to generation. You'll find a variety of sauce *piquantes*, fricassees, stews, casseroles, appetizers, desserts, dressings, breads and breakfast dishes like *couche-couche* and *pain perdu*. Written in clear, easy-to-follow steps. Go ahead, try them, and you, too, will cook like a Cajun! Visit our website to look inside the book and see the list of recipes. 140 RECIPES, 8 ¼ X 10 3/8 IN SIZE, SOFT COVER, ONLY $7.95

CAJUN COUNTRY FUN COLORING & ACTIVITY BOOK

This original book is filled with lively, easy-to-color cartoon characters and scenes from Cajun Country. This book is sure to provide hours of fun and entertainment for your family. It is bilingual, with captions and page numbers written in English and French. Besides the pages to color, the activities include color-by-number, word search, a maze, connect the dots and much more! SOFT COVER, 32 PAGES, $4.95

ORDER FORM

Can't get enough? *Order more copies today!*

FOUR WAYS TO ORDER

Phone Locally call **(337) 224-6576** or call **1-888-60MEALS.**

Web For faster service, order online at **www.RiceCookerMeals.com**
All major credit cards, JCB, debit cards, bank transfers and
PayPal payments.

Fax this completed order form to (337) 237-5644.

Mail Complete form below and mail with check,
money order or credit card authorization to:
Cypress Cove Publishing
Attn: Order Dept. - PO Box 91626, Lafayette, LA 70509-1626

YES! Please RUSH me:

QTY	TITLE	PRICE	S&H
____	*Rice Cooker Meals: Fast Home Cooking for Busy People*	$12.95	$3
____	*Down-Home Cajun Cooking Favorites*	$7.95	$3
____	*Cajun Country Fun Coloring & Activity Book*	$4.95	$3
____	Stainless Steel Rice Cooker	$79.95	$15

for speedy UPS delivery

**NOTE: PLEASE GIVE YOUR STREET ADDRESS FOR RICE COOKER DELIVERY
UPS CANNOT DELIVER TO PO BOXES. THANKS!**

❑ **MAKES A GREAT GIFT!** If you are buying for someone beside yourself
(or in addition to yourself), please check here and write the name and
address of the recipients on a separate sheet of paper.

❑ Enclosed is my check or money order for $_____

❑ Charge $_____ ❑ Visa ❑ MasterCard ❑ AmEx ❑ Discover ❑ JCB

Card # _____ Exp. Date ____/____ 3-digit code _____

Signature _____

Name _____

Address _____

City, State, ZIP _____

Phone _____ email _____

Make check or money order payable to **Cypress Cove Publishing.**
Add $2.00 per copy more for out-of-U.S. orders.